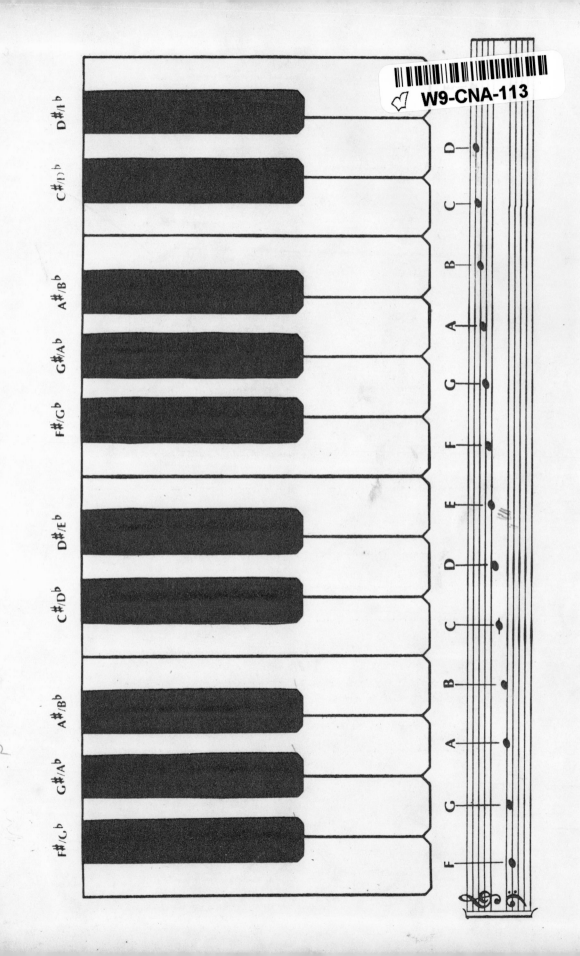

Silver Burdett
music
Centennial Edition

Elizabeth Crook

Bennett Reimer

David S. Walker

SILVER BURDETT COMPANY MORRISTOWN, NEW JERSEY

ATLANTA, GA · CINCINNATI, OH · DALLAS, TX · NORTHFIELD, IL · SAN CARLOS, CA · AGINCOURT, ONTARIO

ISBN 0-382-05925-5

Contents

MOVE TO THE BEAT

1 *Run, Run, Run*

PLAY THE BEAT

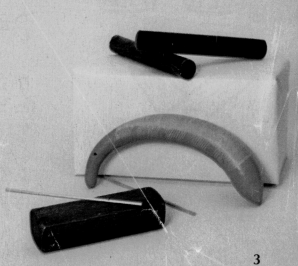

Steady beat:

Quarter notes:

Eighth notes:

Try playing a pattern of quarter notes and eighth notes to accompany *Run, Run, Run*.

PLAY A PATTERN

Pay Me My Money Down

SLAVE SONG FROM THE GEORGIA SEA ISLANDS

COLLECTED AND ADAPTED BY LYDIA A. PARRISH

1. I thought I heard the cap - tain say,

"Pay me my mon - ey down,__

To - mor - row is our sail - ing day,__

Pay me my mon - ey down."_

REFRAIN

"Pay__ me,__ oh, pay__ me,__

Pay me my mon - ey down,__

Pay me or go to jail,__

Pay me my mon - ey down."_

4

2. As soon as the boat was clear of the bar,
   "Pay me my money down,"
   He knocked me down with the end of a spar,
   "Pay me my money down." *Refrain*

3. Well, I wish I was Mr. Steven's son,
   "Pay me my money down,"
   Sit on the bank and watch the work done,
   "Pay me my money down." *Refrain*

CHANT-A-PATTERNS

While someone plays a steady beat on a percussion instrument,

try saying one of these chant-a-patterns.

Make up your own percussion part for "Pay Me My Money Down."
Play it on one of the instruments shown on the opposite page.

How many different rhythm patterns can you think of? The
chant-a-patterns may give you some ideas.

5

Scratch, Scratch

WORDS AND MUSIC BY HARRY BELAFONTE AND LORD BURGESS

A VERSE

1. Oh, we went out to a par - ty,

It was me and Ben and Mac,

And be - fore I knew what hap - pened,

I got an itch - in' on my back.

B REFRAIN

Scratch, scratch me back, Scratch, scratch me back.

It real - ly is a fact,___

The less I itch, the more I scratch.

2. Well, I was quite embarrassed,
Till my two friends I did see,
Well, they were madly itching,
And they were screaming louder than me.
Refrain

3. Now, this scratching was contagious,
And it didn't take very long,
Ev'rybody there was itching,
As they joined me in this song.
Refrain

SETS OF TWO

In this pattern, the quarter notes show beats in sets of two.

Play the pattern along with the tom-tom on the recording.

Hand Game Song
AMERICAN INDIAN SONG

FROM THE RED BOOK OF SINGING GAMES AND DANCES BY JANET E. TOBITT, COPYRIGHT ©, 1960 BY SUMMY-BIRCHARD CO. ALL RIGHTS RESERVED. USED BY PERMISSION.

Ha a a ho - e tha a, Ha a a ho - e tha a

Ha a a ho - e tha a, Ha a ho - e tha,

Ha a a ho - e tha a, Ha a___ a ho - e tha a,

Ha a___ a ho - e tha.

Now try a pattern that uses both quarter notes and eighth notes.

7

HAND JIVE

Try doing a hand jive with this music.

🎯 Scruggs: *String Bender*   🎯 Joplin: *Bethena*

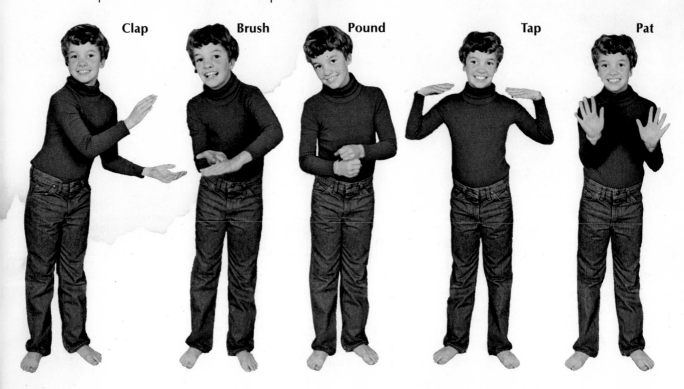

Clap   Brush   Pound   Tap   Pat

Listen to the recording of "Here I Go." Are the beats grouped

in sets of two, or in sets of three?

Here I Go   ROUND 🎯

FROM THE BOOK OF ROUNDS BY MARY CATHERINE TAYLOR AND CAROL DYK. COPYRIGHT © 1977 BY MARY CATHERINE TAYLOR. REPRODUCED BY PERMISSION OF E. P. DUTTON.

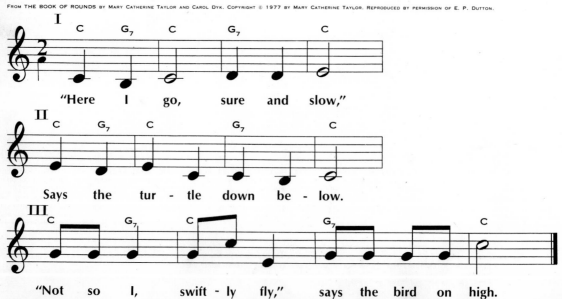

I

"Here   I   go,   sure   and   slow,"

II

Says   the   tur - tle   down   be - low.

III

"Not   so   I,   swift - ly   fly,"   says   the   bird   on   high.

8

SETS OF THREE

Do you know the answer to this riddle? If not, ask someone who does.

When Is a Door?

WORDS AND MUSIC BY GEORGE F. ROOT

When is a door not a door? Give it up?

When is a door not a door? Let me see. Ah,

yes, when it is a - jar.

Sandy McNab

ROUND

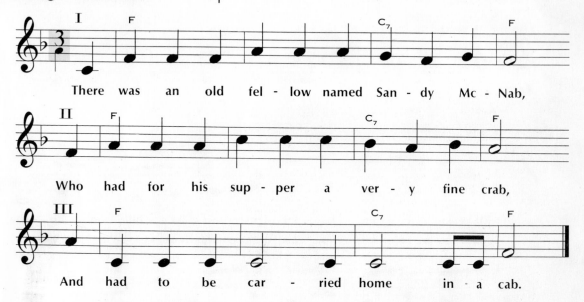

There was an old fel - low named San - dy Mc - Nab,

Who had for his sup - per a ver - y fine crab,

And had to be car - ried home in a cab.

Look at the color box at the beginning of each round. What do you think the number means?

STEPS, LEAPS, REPEATS

Find two G bells, one low and one high. Play the bells, one
after the other, while others sing this folk song from Israel. You
will be playing *octave leaps.*

Hear the Rooster *Kum bahur* FOLK SONG FROM ISRAEL ENGLISH WORDS BY ROSEMARY JACQUES

Hear the roost - er crow - ing, it's time to start the day,
Kum ba - hur a - tzel_____ v' - tzei la - a - vo - da,

Hear the roost - er crow - ing, it's time to start the day.
Kum ba - hur a - tzel_____ v' - tzei la - a - vo - da.

Wake, wake,_____ get up with - out de - lay,
Kum, kum,_____ v' - tzei la - a - vo - da,

Wake, wake,_____ get up with - out de - lay.
Kum, kum,_____ v' - tzei la - a - vo - da.

Ku - ku - ri - ku, ku - ku - ri - ku, let's be on our way,
Ku - ku - ri - ku, ku - ku - ri - ku, tar - n' - gol ka - ra,

Ku - ku - ri - ku, ku - ku - ri - ku, let's be on our way.
Ku - ku - ri - ku, ku - ku - ri - ku, tar - n' - gol ka - ra.

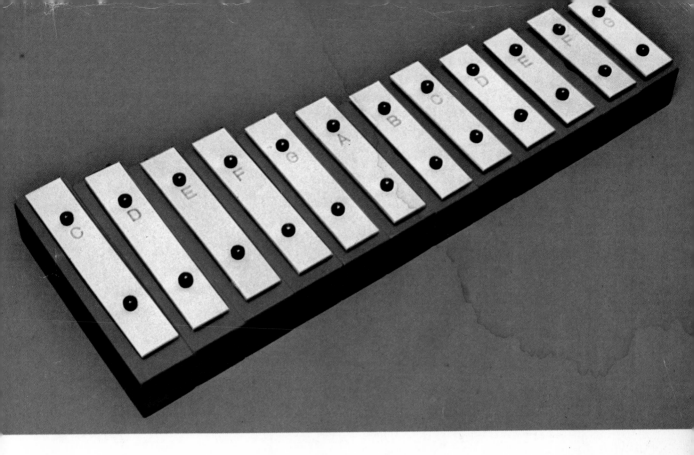

Find repeated tones, leaps, and steps in these bell patterns.

Use your eyes and ears to discover how the tones move in "Hear the Rooster." Follow the notes of the melody as you listen to the recording. Find places where tones *repeat, step,* or *leap.*

NAME THE SONG

These melodies are endings of songs you know.

Can you name the songs?

1.

    F   C

2.

     A   C   F

3.
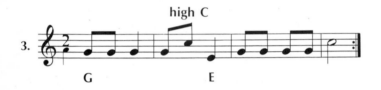
        G   E

"HERE I GO" COUNTERMELODIES

Before you try playing one of the countermelodies on the bells,
figure out how the tones move.

Which countermelody steps mostly downward? Which one uses
an octave leap? Which one has mostly repeated tones?

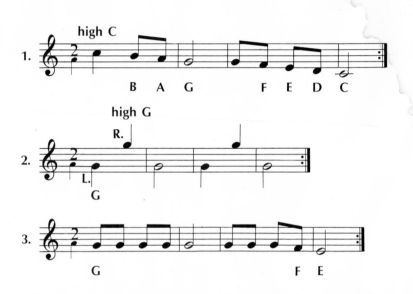

ONE WAY TO MAKE HARMONY

The tones in a melody can move in an upward direction. They can also move in a downward direction. Look at melodies 1 and 2.

1. Hand me down my sil - ver trum-pet, Lord.

2. Hand me down my sil - ver trum-pet, Lord.

If you sing melody 1 and someone else sings melody 2 at the same time, you will be singing in *harmony*.

3. Hand me down my sil - ver trum-pet, Lord.

Look at the notes in the color box. Can you find another place in "Hand Me Down" where upward and downward directions are sung at the same time?

Hand Me Down

BLACK SPIRITUAL

SOLO
C₇   F

Oh,   hand   me down,   Hand   me down,

CHORUS
F   C₇

Hand   me down   my   sil - ver   trum - pet,   Ga - briel.

SOLO

Hand me down, throw it down, An - y way to get it down,

CHORUS

Hand me down my sil - ver trum - pet, Lord.

SOLO

Oh, Mo - ses had a lot to do,___

CHORUS

Hand me down my sil - ver trum - pet, Ga - briel,

SOLO

When he led the chil - dren of Is - ra - el through,

CHORUS

Hand me down my sil - ver trum - pet, Lord.

Sing the chorus parts along with the children's voices on the recording.

Are the chorus parts the same as the solo parts, or different?

Sourwood Mountain

AMERICAN FOLK SONG

SOLO

1. Chick - en crowin' on Sour - wood Moun - tain,
2. My true love's a blue - eyed dai - sy,

CHORUS

Hey de - ing dang did - dle al - ly day.

SOLO

So man - y pret - ty girls, I can't count 'em,
If I don't get her, I'll go cra - zy,

CHORUS

Hey de - ing dang did - dle al - ly day.

SOLO

My true love, she lives in Letch - er,
Big dog bark and little one bite you,

CHORUS

Hey de - ing dang did - dle al - ly day.

SOLO

She won't come and I won't fetch her,
Big girl court and little one slight you,

CHORUS

Hey de - ing dang did - dle al - ly day.

AN AMERICAN SQUARE DANCE

1 ⌒
Honor your partner.

2 ⌒
Honor your corner.

3 ⌒
Change places with partner.

4 ⌒
Come back home.

5 ⌒
Boys to the center.

6 ⌒
Boys back home.

7 ⌒
Girls to the center.

8 ⌒
Girls back home.

Couple 3

Couple 2

Couple 4

Head Couple

TWO SECTIONS— (A) AND B

Listen for the two sections in the recording of this nonsense
song. How is section B different from section A?

Ging Gong Gooli

FOLK SONG FROM BRITISH GUIANA

Ging gong goo-li goo-li goo-li goo-li wat - cha,

Ging gong goo, ging gong goo.

Ging gong goo-li goo-li goo-li goo-li wat - cha,

Ging gong goo, ging gong goo.

Hai - la,_____ hai - la shai - la,_____

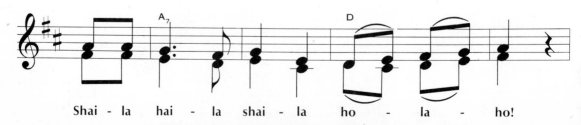

Shai - la hai - la shai - la ho - la - ho!

18

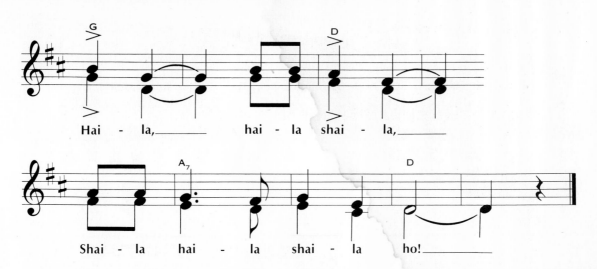

Choose a section of "Ging Gong Gooli" to sing or accompany on a percussion instrument.

THE AUTOHARP

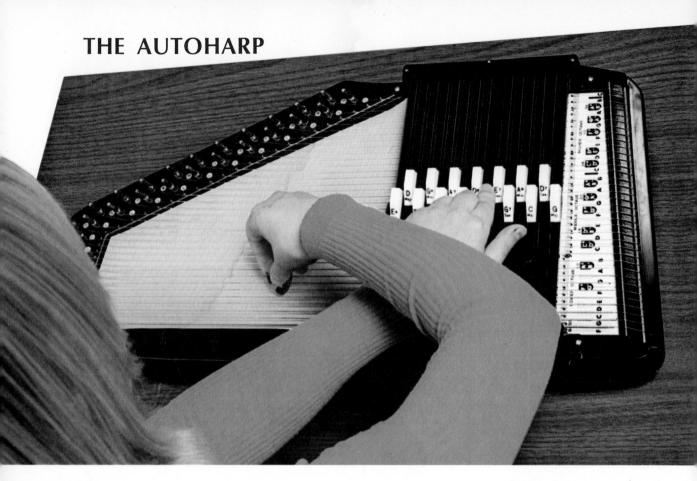

LOOK

LISTEN *The Wise Man Built His House*

PLAY

- Place your left index finger on the button marked F.
- Place your left middle finger on the button marked C₇.
- Look at the chord pattern below. It shows when to press each button.
- As you press the buttons, use your right hand to strum the strings.
- Make each strum last for two beats.
- Follow the chord pattern to play as others sing "The Wise Man Built His House." You will be playing half notes.

20

The Wise Man Built His House

ORIGIN UNKNOWN

1. Oh, the wise man built his house up-on the rock,
2. Oh, the rains came down and the floods came up,

Oh, the wise man built his house up-on the rock,
Oh, the rains came down and the floods came up,

Oh, the wise man built his house up-on the rock,
Oh, the rains came down and the floods came up,

And the rains came tum-bling down.
But the house on the rock stood firm.

3. Oh, the silly man built his house upon the sand, *(3 times)*
   And the rains came tumbling down.

4. Oh, the rains came down and the floods came up, *(3 times)*
   And the house on the sand went swissssssssssh.

Use the Autoharp to accompany other two-chord songs you know.

- "Pay Me My Money Down," page 4
- "Here I Go," page 8
- "Hear the Rooster," page 10
- "Hand Me Down," page 14

AUTOHARP AND PERCUSSION

Listen to the recording of "Sambalele." The Autoharp plays this chord pattern all through the song.

What other instruments do you hear on the recording?

Sambalele FOLK SONG FROM BRAZIL   WORDS BY RUTH AND THOMAS MARTIN

A VERSE

1. Hear how the mu - sic is play - ing,
2. Dance while the drum - beat is pound - ing,

Dance to its light - heart - ed mea - sures,
Mel - low gui - tars soft - ly strum - ming,

Clap - ping and stamp - ing and sway - ing,
And cas - ta - nets clear - ly sound - ing,

Join in the car - ni - val plea - sures.
Join in the whis - tling and hum - ming.

B REFRAIN

Sam - ba, sam - ba, sam - ba - la - le - le,

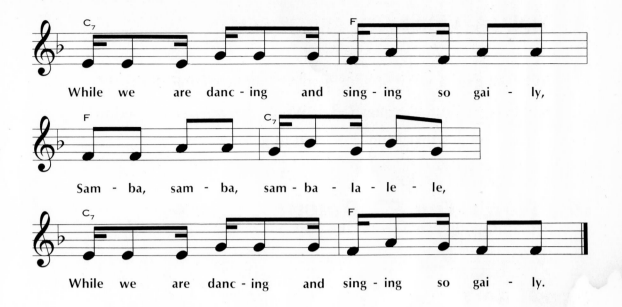

While we are danc-ing and sing-ing so gai - ly,

Sam - ba, sam - ba, sam-ba - la - le - le,

While we are danc - ing and sing-ing so gai - ly.

PICK A PART

Make up your own accompaniment for "Sambalele." Add one
or two of these parts to the Autoharp pattern.

Section A

Castanets
or Maraca

Section B

Bongos

Cowbell

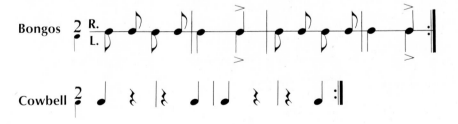

Section A or B

Voices
and Bells

C   A   B♭ G   B♭ G   A   F

Sam-ba, sam-ba, sam - ba; Sam-ba, sam-ba, sam - ba.

ADD A VERSE

Try making up a verse of your own to sing in section B. You
might start with these questions: "Who's that yonder dressed in
green?" "Who's that yonder dressed in gold?"

Oh, Won't You Sit Down? BLACK SPIRITUAL

(A) REFRAIN

SOLO   G   CHORUS   D₇

Oh, won't you sit down?__ Lord, I can't sit down.__

SOLO   G   CHORUS   D₇

Oh, won't you sit down?__ Lord, I can't sit down.__

SOLO   G   CHORUS   D₇

Oh, won't you sit down?__ Lord, I can't sit down.__

G   D₇   G   Fine

'Cause I just got to Heav-en, gon-na look a - round.__

B VERSE

G SOLO

1. Who's that yon - der dressed in red?__

CHORUS

G   D₇   G

Must be the chil-dren that__ Mo - ses led.__

24

Who's that yon - der dressed in white? __

CHORUS

Must be the chil - dren of the Is - rael - ite. ____

2. Who's that yonder dressed in blue?

Must be the children that are comin' through.

Who's that yonder dressed in black?

Must be the hypocrites a-turnin' back. *Refrain*

PUT IT ALL TOGETHER

Section A

Sit down, Broth-er. Sit down, Broth-er.

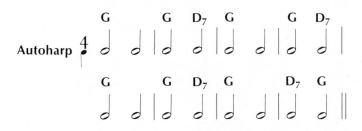

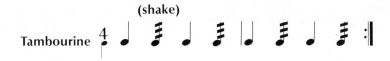

Section B

Play during chorus parts only.

THE RECORDER

LOOK

LISTEN

Listen to the tone color
of a group of recorders,
called a consort.

Widmann, Erasmus: *Margaretha*

26

PLAY

G

G

How to Play G

1. Using your left hand, cover the holes shown in the diagram.

   Press just hard enough so the holes make a light mark on your fingers.

2. Cover the tip of the mouthpiece with your lips. Blow gently

   as you whisper "daah."

Play G throughout a song you know.

🔘 *Hear the Rooster,* Version 2
1

Now try playing G, A, and B.

Your recorder notes look like this.

Your fingers should cover these holes.

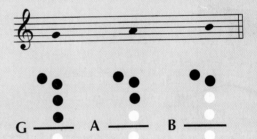

G — A — B

Play a recorder part for "Ging Gong Gooli." It uses G, A, B.

Ⓐ

A   G

Ⓑ

B

THREE-NOTE RECORDER MELODIES

Practice playing some melodies that use B, A, G on the recorder.

Hot Cross Buns
TRADITIONAL

Hot cross buns, Hot cross buns,

One a pen - ny, two a pen - ny, Hot cross buns.

At Pierrot's Door
FOLK MELODY FROM FRANCE

In the sil - v'ry moon - light, Tap - ping at your door,
In the sil - v'ry moon - light, Sleep - y Pier - rot said,

I have come, good neigh - bor, Twen - ty miles or more.
"No, I will not o - pen, I have gone to bed."

Merrily We Roll Along
TRADITIONAL

Mer - ri - ly we roll a - long, Roll a - long, Roll a - long,

Mer - ri - ly we roll a - long, O'er the deep blue sea.

MORE THINGS TO DO WITH B A G

Play the melodies on page 28 for your friends. You might want to ask someone to accompany you on the Autoharp.

All three melodies use the chords G and D_7. Let your ears tell you when to change from one chord to another.

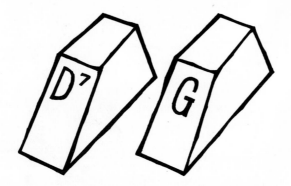

Here are two countermelodies to play with a song you know— "Oh, Won't You Sit Down?" page 24. The first countermelody is for section A; the second, for section B.

SING THE RHYMES

How many words can you think of to rhyme with Michael's last name?

Sing the ones in this song.

Michael Finnegan

CHILDREN'S GAME SONG

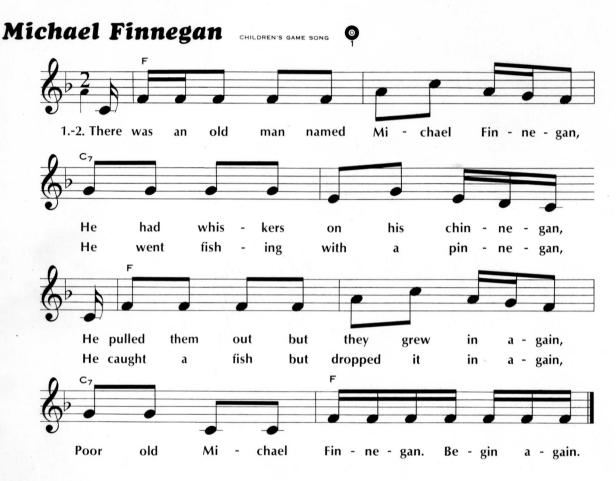

1.-2. There was an old man named Mi - chael Fin - ne - gan,

He had whis - kers on his chin - ne - gan,
He went fish - ing with a pin - ne - gan,

He pulled them out but they grew in a - gain,
He caught a fish but dropped it in a - gain,

Poor old Mi - chael Fin - ne - gan. Be - gin a - gain.

3. There was an old man named Michael Finnegan,
   Climbed a tree and barked his shinnegan,
   He lost about a yard of skinnegan,
   Poor old Michael Finnegan. Begin again.

4. There was an old man named Michael Finnegan,
   He grew fat and then grew thinnegan,
   Then he died and that's the endegan,
   Poor old Michael Finnegan. Begin again.

Make up another verse about poor old Michael Finnegan.

TWO WAYS TO SING A SONG

NO HARMONY

When you sing a melody alone, there is no harmony.

This drawing shows a melody alone.

Sing "Michael Finnegan" as a melody alone.

HARMONY

When you play chords to accompany a melody, there is harmony.

This drawing shows a melody with chords.

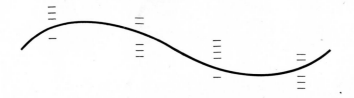

Sing "Michael Finnegan" with an Autoharp accompaniment.

Here are the chords to play.

TWO WAYS TO MAKE HARMONY

When chords accompany a melody, there is harmony.

Choose a song you know and play the Autoharp chords to accompany your singing.

Two melodies that fit together also make harmony.
This drawing shows melodies together.

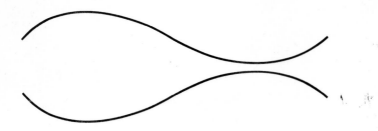

Here is a melody that fits together with "Michael Finnegan."

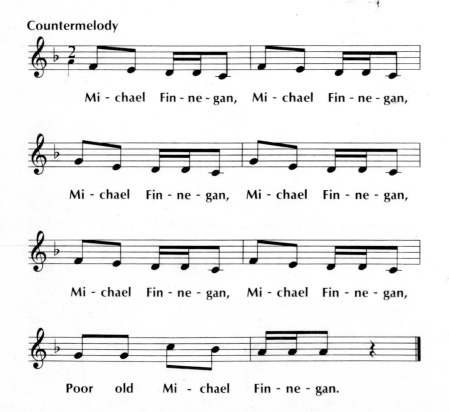

Listen to these pieces.

For each one, choose the symbol that best describes the texture.

If you hear melody alone, choose  .

If you hear melody with chords, choose  .

If you hear two or more melodies together, choose  .

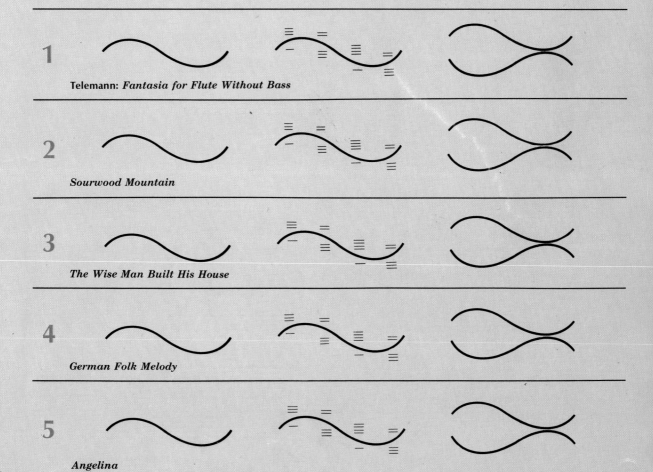

1   Telemann: *Fantasia for Flute Without Bass*

2   *Sourwood Mountain*

3   *The Wise Man Built His House*

4   *German Folk Melody*

5   *Angelina*

Listening to Music

What part of you lets you hear the sounds of this music?

CALL CHART 1: Listening To Music

As your ears hear sounds, your mind tells you what the sounds are doing. How many of these things is your mind aware of? The numbers will help you listen carefully.

Bizet: *L'Arlésienne Suite No. 1*, Overture

1 *THEME:* **Strings play together.**

2 *VARIATION 1:* **Soft; woodwinds play.**

3 *VARIATION 2:* **Gets louder and softer.**

4 *VARIATION 3:* **Slower; theme smooth; accompaniment has short tones.**

5 *VARIATION 4:* **Like a march; drums play.**

6 *CODA (ending section):* **Loud, soft, ends softly.**

The more _sounds_ your _ears hear_, and the more sounds your _mind_ is _aware_ of, the more your _feelings_ can _respond_.

An orchestra is making the sounds of this music.

Paintings give a feeling of movement.

Which painting seems to be more active?

Which painting seems to be more still?

Why?

Music also gives a feeling of movement. Which piece seems to be more active? Which piece seems to be more still?

◎ Gershwin: *An American in Paris*
2

◎ Ives: *The Pond*
2

Both painting and music seem to have movement. Some paintings and some music have active movement—others are still. Each art creates a sense of movement differently, so each art gives its own special feeling.

Tempo

FOLLOW-THE-TEMPO GAME

When it's your turn to be leader, make up your own "tempo plan" for "Flea!" Will you start fast? Slow? Will the tempo get faster? Will it get slower? Or what?

Clapping Pattern:

CHANGING TEMPO

Follow the tempo of the music. Does it get faster? Slower?

Dayenu
HEBREW PASSOVER SONG   ENGLISH WORDS BY ELIZABETH S. BACHMAN

(A) VERSE

1. He has led us out of E - gypt, led His peo - ple out of E - gypt,

He has led us out of E - gypt, da - ye - nu.

(B) REFRAIN   *gradually getting faster (accelerando)*

Da - da - ye - nu,_____ da - da - ye - nu,_____

Da - da - ye - nu, da - ye - nu da - ye - nu da - ye - nu,

Da - da - ye - nu,_____ da - da - ye - nu,_____

Da - da - ye - nu, da - ye - nu da - ye - nu.

2. He has given us the Sabbath, given us the holy Sabbath,

   He has given us the Sabbath, *dayenu. Refrain*

3. He has given us the Torah, given us the blessed Torah,

   He has given us the Torah, *dayenu. Refrain*

40

FOLLOW THE TEMPO

If you felt lazier and lazier would you move faster and faster, or slower and slower?

How does the tempo change in this song? To find out, listen to the recording.

Lazy Coconut Tree

MUSIC BY DOUGLAS COOMBES   WORDS BY JOHN EMLYN EDWARDS

FROM TA-RA-RA-BOOM-DE-AY. PUBLISHED BY A & C BLACK LTD. REPRINTED BY PERMISSION OF DAVID HIGHAM ASSOCIATES LIMITED.

1. Some folk like to go fish - ing____ far a - cross the bay,
2. I could be a rich mer - chant____ in some fine ba - zaar,

I would rath - er be dream - ing____ on the beach all day.
But I'd rath - er be hap - py____ nod - ding to a star.

(optional harmony part)*

Like the la - zy co - co - co - co-nut, co - co - co - co-nut tree,

gradually getting slower (rallentando)

Like the la - zy co - co - co - co-nut, co - co - co - co-nut tree.

Maracas

Bongos

Claves

THREE SECTIONS—THREE TEMPOS

This song has three sections—A, B, C. How is the tempo different in each one?

Dry Bones
BLACK SPIRITUAL

E - ze - kiel cried,"Them dry bones!" E - ze - kiel cried,"Them dry bones!"

E - ze - kiel cried,"Them dry bones!" Now hear the word of the Lord.

B gradually getting faster

The foot bone con - nect - ed to the leg bone,

The leg bone con - nect - ed to the knee bone,

The knee bone con - nect - ed to the hip bone,

The hip bone con - nect - ed to the back bone,

The back bone con - nect - ed to the shoul - der bone,

The shoul - der bone con - nect - ed to the neck bone,

The neck bone con-nect-ed to the jaw bone,

The jaw bone con-nect-ed to the head bone,

Now hear the word of the Lord.

C fast

Them bones, them bones gon-na walk a-round, Them bones, them bones gon-na

walk a-round, Them bones, them bones gon-na walk a-round,

getting slower last time

Now hear the word of the Lord.

CALL CHART 2: Tempo

Listen for the tempo in these pieces. As each number is called,

look at the chart. It will help you hear what the beat is doing.

Satie: *Sports et Divertissements*

1 *SLOW* ("CHANT")		**4** *FAST* ("THE HUNT")
2 *FAST* ("FIREWORKS")		**5** *MODERATE* ("FISHING")
3 *MODERATE* ("SEE-SAW")		

FANCY STEPPING

Some music makes you want to move to the beat.

Try some "fancy stepping" with this song.

I'm Gonna Walk

WORDS AND MUSIC BY DAVID EDDLEMAN

I'm gon-na put, put, put on my walk-in' shoes, I'm gon-na

but-, but-, but-ton up my coat, I'm gon-na

walk right a-cross the land, there's lots o' things to see, And if you

wan-ta you can walk with me.___ Oh, yes, I'm gon-na

walk to the East,___ Walk to the West,___

Walk to the North and South;___ The

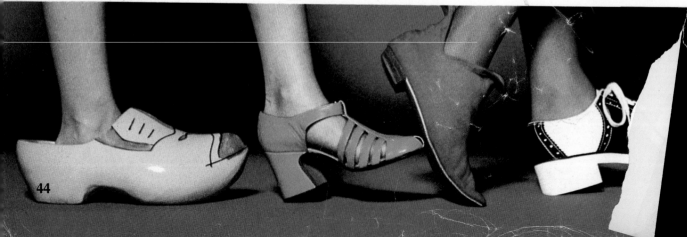

44

one thing that I love ____ the best ____ Is

walk - in' all a - bout. ____ Well, ____ I'm gon - na

put, put, put on my walk - in' shoes, I'm gon - na

but-, but-, but - ton up my coat, I'm gon - na

walk right a - cross the land, there's lots o' things to see, And if you

wan - ta you can walk with me, ____ Walk with me, ____

Walk with me, ____ Walk with ____ me.

Find the sign in the music that tells you the beat stops and holds.

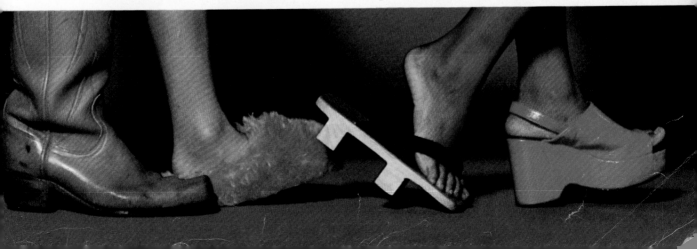

Select a tempo by chance.   **Select a time span by chance.**

fast   slow   moderate   5″   10″   15″   20″

10″	15″	5″	20″

Example:

        fast   moderate   slow   moderate

Play a section from a cassette tape in the tempo
and time span you have chosen.

To perform a complete piece with others, select
the order, by chance, in which you will play.

WHAT DO YOU HEAR?   2: Tempo ⊙₂

Each time a number is called, decide which of the two answers is correct.

Choose the answer that best describes what is happening in the music.

Dvořák: *Slavonic Dances*, Op. 46, No. 7

1	FAST	SLOW
2	GETTING FASTER	GETTING SLOWER
3	FAST	SLOW
4	GETTING FASTER	GETTING SLOWER
5	FAST	SLOW

Stravinsky: *Fireworks*

1	FAST	SLOW
2	FASTER	SLOWER
3	GETTING FASTER	GETTING SLOWER

WHAT DO YOU HEAR?   3: Tempo ⊙₂

Choose the word that best describes the tempo. Is it fast, or slow?

Do you hear the beat stop and hold? If you do, choose the fermata sign ⌒.

If you do not, choose no ⌒.

1	FAST ⌒	SLOW NO ⌒	Haydn: *Symphony No. 104*, Movement 1
2	FAST ⌒	SLOW NO ⌒	Beethoven: *Violin Concerto*, Movement 3
3	FAST ⌒	SLOW NO ⌒	*Weary of the Railway*

Careers in Music:
Compose, Perform

Hale Smith

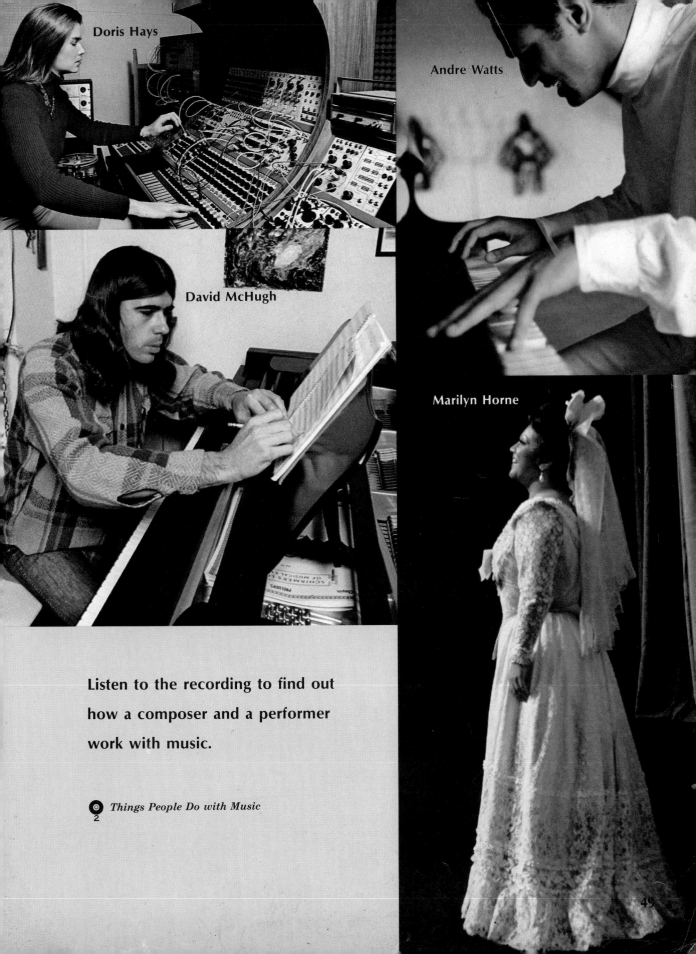

Doris Hays

Andre Watts

David McHugh

Marilyn Horne

Listen to the recording to find out
how a composer and a performer
work with music.

Things People Do with Music
2

DIRECTION

With the tip of one finger, trace the outline made by the edge of the mountain. Notice that your finger goes upward and downward.

Now trace the outline made by the arrow drawings.

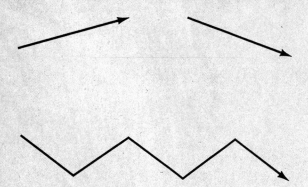

Play the tones that each arrow drawing suggests on the bells or on the keyboard.

In music, *notation* shows direction. How do the tones move in these three little melodies?

1.
G
Sit down, Broth - er,

2.
C
Hand me down my sil - ver trum-pet, Lord.

3.
D
Pay me or go to jail,— Pay me my mon-ey down."

AN ADD-ON SONG

The old lady in this song has a special appetite. When you catch on to the form, join in with the recording.

I Know an Old Lady

MUSIC BY ALAN MILLS   WORDS BY ROSE BONNE

COPYRIGHT 1952 AND 1960 BY PEER INTERNATIONAL (CANADA) LTD. SOLE SELLING AGENT PEER INTERNATIONAL CORPORATION. USED BY PERMISSION.

1. I know an old la - dy who swal-lowed a fly; I don't know why she swal-lowed a fly! I guess she'll die. _____ 2. I

know an old la - dy who swal-lowed a spi - der that wrig-gled and wrig-gled and tick-led in - side her; She swal-lowed the spi - der to catch the fly, But I don't know why she swal-lowed the fly. I guess she'll die! _____ I

know an old la - dy who swal-lowed a

bird! Now, how ab - surd, to
cat! Now, fan - cy that, to
dog! My, what a hog, to
goat! Just opened her throat and
cow! I don't know how she

swal - low   a   bird!   3. She swal-lowed the bird   to   catch   the   spi - der
swal - low   a   cat!   4. She swal-lowed the cat   to   catch   the   bird,__ (*To 3*)
swal - low   a   dog!   5. She swal-lowed the dog   to   catch   the   cat, __ (*To 4*)
swal-lowed a goat!   6. She swal-lowed the goat   to   catch   the   dog,__ (*To 5*)
swal-lowed a cow!   7. She swal-lowed the cow   to   catch   the   goat,__ (*To 6*)

that wrig-gled and wrig-gled and tick-led   in - side her, She swal-lowed the spi-der to

catch   the   fly,   But   I   don't know why   she swal-lowed the fly;

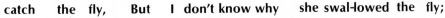

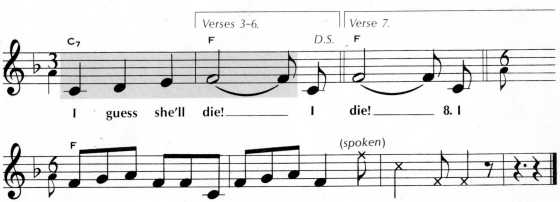

I   guess   she'll   die!_____   I   die! _____   8. I

Know   an   old   la - dy who swal-lowed a horse; She's dead,   of course!

Here are two ways to play and sing part of the song.

Which staff shows tones that move upward? Downward?

1.

C   D   E   F
I guess she'll die._____

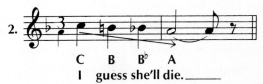

2.

C   B   B♭   A
I guess she'll die._____

Fisherman's Song

CALYPSO MELODY   WORDS BY WILLIAM ATTAWAY

(A) VERSE

1. Fish - er - men   sleep   when the   fish don't   bite,____
2. Fish - er - man's   la - dy don't use   no   comb,____

Weigh   up,   Sus - i - an - na,

Salt fish   in   the hold   and we   two ton   light,____
She comb her____   hair   with____   cod - fish   bone,____

Round   the Bay   of   Mont - ser - ray.____

(B) REFRAIN

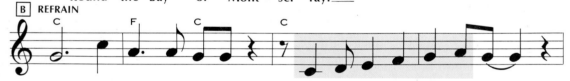

Weigh   up,   Sus - i - an - na,   Round the Bay   of Mont - ser - ray.____

Fish   all____   night   and   we   sleep   all   day,____

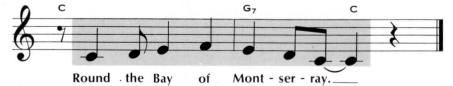

Round . the Bay   of   Mont - ser - ray.____

3. Fisherman's lady got a dimple knee,

Weigh up, Susianna,

She boil her porgy with rice and peas,

Round the Bay of Montserray. *Refrain*

54

A POEM SET TO MUSIC

The poet who wrote the words of this song saw white sheep walking across the sky. Use your voice to create this special feeling about clouds.

Clouds

MUSIC BY HOAGY CARMICHAEL   WORDS BY CHRISTINA ROSSETTI

White sheep, white sheep, high on a wind - y hill,

When _____ the wind stops, you all stand still;

But___ when_____ the wind blows, you walk a - way slow.

Oh, white sheep, white sheep, where do you go?

Countermelody 1

high C

B   A   G   F   E   D

Countermelody 2

A   G   F   E   D   C

55

CONTOUR—THE SHAPE OF A MELODY

How would you feel if your best friend moved away?

Let your voice express this feeling when you sing about Louis.

Louis Moved Away

MUSIC BY JIM HUNTER   WORDS BY TOM PAISLEY

Lou - is___ moved___ a - way to - day;___

Lou - is___ was___ my___ friend.___

Him and___ me___ would al - ways___ play,___

He al - ways had some bread to___ spend.___

His dad - dy makes good___ pay;___

That's what they all___ say.___

And now I'll nev - er have a___ friend,___

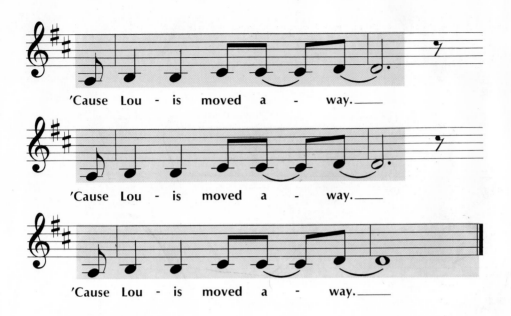

'Cause Lou - is moved a - way.____

'Cause Lou - is moved a - way.____

'Cause Lou - is moved a - way.____

The way tones move gives a melody its shape. Another word for "shape" is *contour.*

Follow the contour of the melody as you sing the song again. Which phrases move mostly downward? Mostly upward?

Play the last three phrases on bells or piano. They start on low A. In which direction will you play?

Listen for direction in this piano piece. You will hear places where the pianist plays downward from one end of the keyboard to the other.

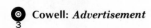 Cowell: *Advertisement*

Doris Hays is the performer on this recording of *Advertisement.* You will find her picture on page 49.

When the Saints Go Marching In

BLACK SPIRITUAL

As you sing this song, let your voice do the marching.

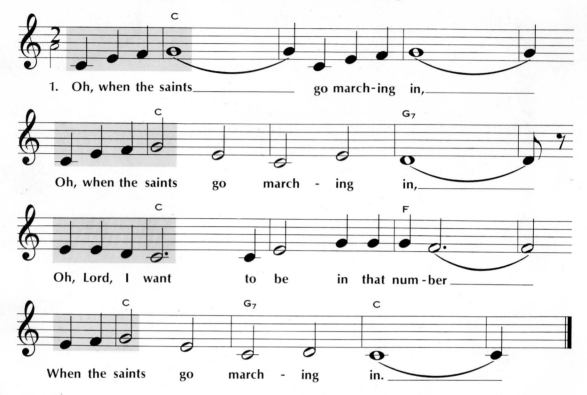

1. Oh, when the saints_____ go march-ing in,_____

Oh, when the saints go march - ing in,_____

Oh, Lord, I want to be in that num-ber_____

When the saints go march - ing in.

2. Oh, when the stars refuse to shine, . . .   3. Oh, when I hear that trumpet sound, . . .

The beginning of each phrase is shown in a color box. Do most phrases begin with tones that move upward, or downward?

This recorder part uses notes you know—B, A, and G. Play the part as others sing the song.

Recorder or Bells

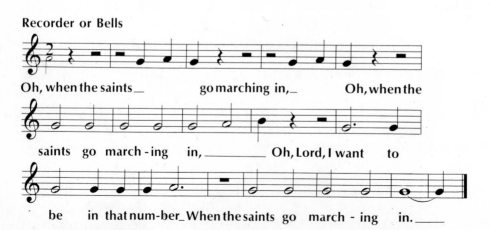

Oh, when the saints_ go marching in,_ Oh, when the

saints go march - ing in, _____ Oh, Lord, I want to

be in that num-ber_ When the saints go march - ing in. ___

58

MATCHING THE CONTOUR

Find other places in the song that match the contour of the phrases in the color boxes.

Harvest Time

WORDS AND MUSIC BY GRACE C. NASH

FROM MUSIC WITH CHILDREN, JUNIOR CHOIR WITH ORFF INSTRUMENTS BY MURRAY McNAIR AND GRACE C. NASH, BY SPECIAL PERMISSION OF GRACE C. NASH.

Har - vest is the sea - son to be - hold.

Har - vest with its col - ors brown and gold.

Crops are in and sum - mer work is done.

Air is crisp and snow is soon to come.

Har - vest is the sea - son to be - hold.

TWO NEW NOTES

E   D

Ostinato 1

Ostinato 2

Drum Ostinato

59

I Love the Mountains

TRADITIONAL

The melody of this song seems to climb right up the mountain.
Make your voice "bounce" with the beat along with the voices
on the recording.

Sing this part over and over throughout the song.

Boom, boom, boom, boom-dee-ah - da

SOUND PIECE 2: Contours at the Keyboard DAVID S. WALKER

Can you figure out how to play this piece on a keyboard?

What do you think the symbols mean?

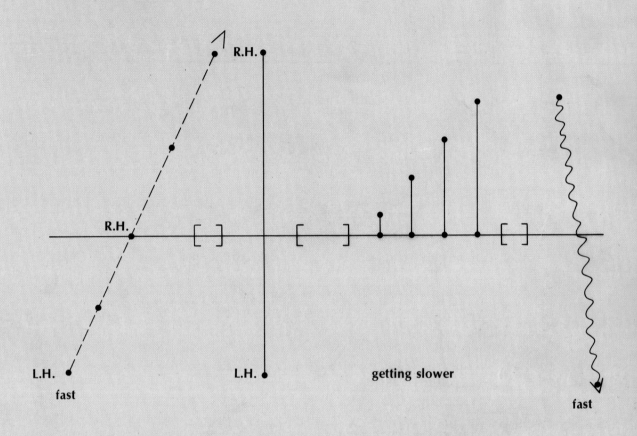

Be a melody detective. Here is the contour of the first phrase of

a patriotic song. Can you guess what it is?

For the answer, turn the page.

The Star-Spangled Banner

MUSIC BY JOHN STAFFORD SMITH   WORDS BY FRANCIS SCOTT KEY

Find other places in the song that match the contour of the
phrases in the color boxes.

Oh,___ say! can you see, by the dawn's ear - ly light,

What so proud - ly we hailed at the twi - light's last gleam - ing,

Whose broad stripes and bright stars, through the per - il - ous fight,

O'er the ram - parts we watched were so gal - lant - ly stream - ing?

And the rock - ets' red glare, the bombs burst - ing in air,

Gave proof through the night that our flag was still there.

Oh, say, does that___ Star - Span - gled Ban - ner___ yet___ wave___

O'er the land___ of the free and the home of the brave.

CALL CHART 3: Direction ⊚₃

Trace the upward and downward arrows with your finger each time you hear section A. The arrows show how the violin swoops upward and downward.

Paganini: *Caprice No. 5 in A Minor*, Op. 1

---

1 SECTION A (UPWARD THEN DOWNWARD)

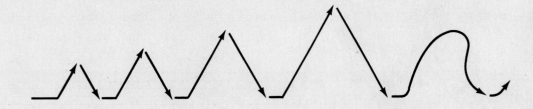

---

2 SECTION B (BOTH UPWARD AND DOWNWARD)

---

3 SECTION A REPEATS.

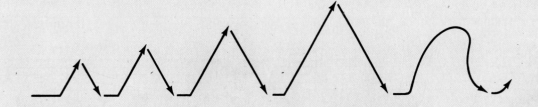

UPWARD, OR DOWNWARD?

How does the melody move when you sing the words *Go, tell it on the mountain?*

Go, Tell It on the Mountain

BLACK SPIRITUAL

Ⓐ VERSE

Freely

1. When I was a seek - er, I sought both night and day.
2. He made me a watch-man Up - on the cit - y wall.
3. In the time of Da - vid, Some said he was a king.

I asked the Lord to help me, And He shows me the way.____
And if I serve Him tru - ly, I am the least of all.____
And if a child is true born, The Lord will hear him sing.____

Ⓑ REFRAIN *(in rhythm)*

Go, tell it on the moun-tain, O - ver__ the hills and ev - 'ry - where.

COUNTERMELODY

Go, tell it on the moun-tain,

Go, tell it on the moun-tain, Our heav'n - ly Lord____ is born.

Go, tell it on the moun-tain, our Lord is born.

Listen to these pieces. Choose the answer that describes the direction in which the melody is mostly moving.

---

1 *UPWARD* *DOWNWARD* *BOTH UPWARD AND DOWNWARD*

Beethoven: *Symphony No. 1*, Movement 1

---

2 *UPWARD* *DOWNWARD* *BOTH UPWARD AND DOWNWARD*

The Star-Spangled Banner

---

3 *UPWARD* *DOWNWARD* *BOTH UPWARD AND DOWNWARD*

Poulenc: *Mouvement Perpétuel No. 1*

---

4 *UPWARD* *DOWNWARD* *BOTH UPWARD AND DOWNWARD*

Cowell: *Advertisement*

---

5 *UPWARD* *DOWNWARD* *BOTH UPWARD AND DOWNWARD*

Mussorgsky: *Pictures at an Exhibition:* "The Little Hut on Chicken's Legs"

---

6 *UPWARD* *DOWNWARD* *BOTH UPWARD AND DOWNWARD*

Paganini: *Caprice No. 5 in A Minor*

Style: Same, or Different?

Do the poems on these pages
look as if they are in the same
style, or in different styles?

Follow the words in each poem
as you listen to the recording.

CROSSING 🔘
3

STOP   LOOK   LISTEN
  as gate stripes swing down,
    count the cars hauling distance
    upgrade through town:
      warning whistle, bellclang,
        engine eating steam,
        engineer waving,
          a fast-freight dream:
          B&M boxcar,
            boxcar again,   FIFTY-NINE, SIXTY,
            Frisco gondola,   hoppers of coke,
EIGHT-NINE-TEN,   Anaconda copper,
  Erie and Wabash,   hotbox smoke,
    Seaboard, U.P.,   EIGHTY-EIGHT,
    Pennsy tankcar,   red-ball freight,
TWENTY-TWO, THREE,   Rio Grande,
  Phoebe Snow, B&O,   Nickel Plate,
THIRTY-FOUR, FIVE,   Hiawatha,
  Santa Fe cattle   Lackawanna,
    shipped alive,   rolling fast
    red cars, yellow cars,   and loose,
      orange cars, black,   NINETY-SEVEN,
        Youngstown steel   coal car,
        down to Mobile   boxcar,
          on Rock Island track,   CABOOSE!

66   Philip Booth

SLOWLY 🎯
3

Slowly the tide creeps up the sand,
Slowly the shadows cross the land.
Slowly the cart-horse pulls his mile,
Slowly the old man mounts the stile.

Slowly the hands move round the clock,
Slowly the dew dries on the dock.
Slow is the snail—but slowest of all
The green moss spreads on the old brick wall.

James Reeves

Poems can be in different styles. Music can be in different styles, too.
Listen to these pieces to discover the differences between them—
the things that tell you they are in different styles.

🎯 Mozart: *Cassation in B♭*, Menuetto No. 1
3

🎯 Schoenberg: *Five Pieces for Orchestra*, No. 1
3

How many things can you hear that make the style of one piece
different from that of the other?

There are different ways of planning poems and music to create
different styles. Each style has its own special way of feeling.

Meter

TWOS, OR THREES?

Are the beats in this singing game from Africa grouped in sets
of two, or in sets of three?

Sasa Aberewa   SINGING GAME FROM AFRICA

FROM AFRICAN SONGS AND GAMES FOR CHILDREN COMPILED AND TRANSCRIBED BY KOJO FOSU BAIDEN AND GERALDINE SLAUGHTER. © 1970, KOJO FOSU BAIDEN AND GERALDINE SLAUGHTER.

Sa   s'a bere wa   o de hyee, Sa   s'a bere wa   o de hyee.
(Sah   sah bray wah hoh dee shee, Sah   sah bray wah   hoh dee shee.)

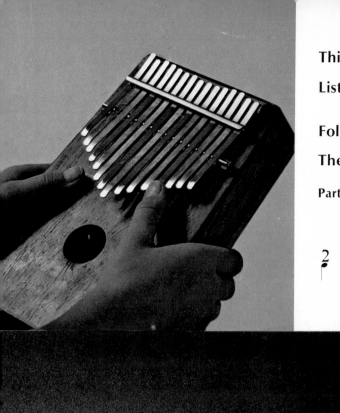

This song is usually accompanied on a kalimba.

Listen for the kalimba sound on the recording.

Follow these directions to play the singing game.

The pictures will help you learn the motions.

Partners face each other with hands stretched out.
 The left palms are turned upward,
 the right palms are turned downward.

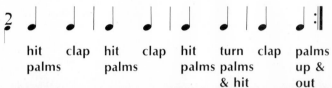

| hit palms | clap | hit palms | clap | hit palms | turn palms & hit | clap | palms up & out |

TWOS, OR THREES?

Find the Ring

FOLK SONG FROM GREECE   ENGLISH WORDS BY MARIA JORDAN

(optional harmony part)

1. Find the ring, the ring that keeps mov - ing,
2. Find the ring, the ring that keeps mov - ing,

Find the ring, oh, where did it go?
Find the ring of sil - ver or gold.

The se - cret ring's in some - bod - y's hand, Some -
Pass it to me, I'll pass it to you, We

bod - y you know, come guess if you can!
must - n't get caught, what - ev - er we do!

Don't say a word if you are the one, Don't

give it a - way and spoil all the fun!

FIND-THE-RING GAME

Form a circle and follow these motions to pass the ring from one to the other.

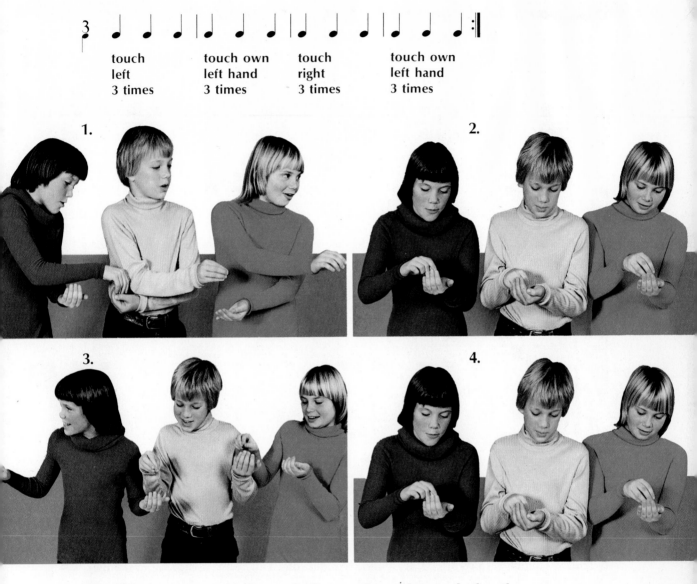

touch
left
3 times

touch own
left hand
3 times

touch
right
3 times

touch own
left hand
3 times

Play this part on recorder or bells as others sing and play the game.

Recorder or Bells

SOUND PIECE 3: Did Sid?

DORIS HAYS   © 1979 DORIS HAYS

SOUND PIECE 4: Busy Lizzy

DORIS HAYS   © 1979 DORIS HAYS

Liz was so bus-y, she was diz-zy,

Bus-y Liz-zy, Bus-y Liz-zy,   Bus-y Liz-zy, Bus-y Liz-zy, Bus-y Liz-zy,

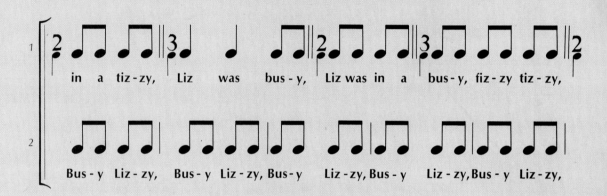

in a tiz-zy, Liz was bus-y, Liz was in a bus-y, fiz-zy tiz-zy,

Bus-y Liz-zy, Bus-y Liz-zy, Bus-y Liz-zy, Bus-y Liz-zy, Bus-y Liz-zy,

Bus-y Liz-zy!

Bus-y Liz-zy.

METER IN 3

Feel meter in 3 by playing this tambourine part with the recording.

Tambourine

(shake)

Mañana

FOLK SONG FROM SPAIN   COLLECTED AND ADAPTED BY BEATRICE LANDECK   ENGLISH WORDS BY ROSEMARY JACQUES

Ma - ña - na, por_____ la ma - ña - na pa -
Ma - ña - na, por_____ la ma - ña - na I_____

sas - te, Jua - na, por_____ mi ta - ller, la ran le.
stood there, Look - ing down_____ at the street, la ran le.

Te ju - ro que_____ ten - go ga - na de_____
When Juana passed by_____ with her twin - kling eye,_____

ver - te, Jua - na, la_____ pun - ta el pie._____
I just saw the toes_____ of her feet._____

Here are two other patterns to use with the song.

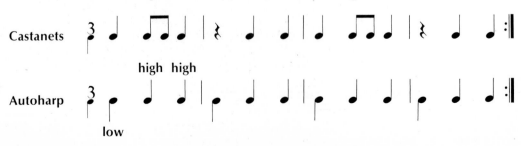

Castanets

high high

Autoharp

METER IN 4

Feel meter in 4 by strumming this low-high pattern on the Autoharp.

FOLK SONG FROM NEWFOUNDLAND

FROM OLD TIME SONGS AND POETRY OF NEWFOUNDLAND. REPRINTED BY PERMISSION OF GERALD S. DOYLE LTD.

SOLO   F   C₇   CHORUS   F

1. A great big sea hove in Long Beach, Right fol - or - al
2. A great big sea hove in the Harbor,

C₇   SOLO   F   C₇

tad - dle did - dle I - do.   A great big sea hove in Long Beach And
                                A great big sea hove in the Harbor And

C₇   C₇   CHORUS F   C₇   F

Gran - ny Snooks she lost her speech, To me right fol - di - dy fol - dee.
hove right up in Ke - ough's Parlor,

3. "Oh, mother dear, I wants a sack,"

Right fol-or-al taddle diddle I-do.

"Oh, mother dear, I wants a sack

With beads and buttons down the back,"

To me right fol-didy fol-dee.

Play these four-meter patterns on the low- and high-C bells.

high C

1.

low C

2.

3.

DANCE IN FOURS: SCHOTTISCHE

PLAY

Play beats in sets of four on a wood block.

Make the first beat of each set stronger than the others.

Now practice making the fourth beat silent.

Wood Block
Pattern

Play the wood block pattern along with the recording.

🔘 *Balkan Hills Schottische*
3

You have played the rhythm of a dance called the *schottische.*

DANCE

To dance a schottische, walk forward on the first three beats of
the measure and hop on the fourth beat. Begin with either
foot. Make your movements match the meter of the music.

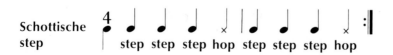

Schottische
step

step step step hop step step step hop

Vary the schottische step this way.

step hop step hop step hop step hop

DANCE IN THREES: MAZURKA

PLAY

Play beats in sets of three on a tambourine. Make the first beat of each set stronger than the others.

Now shake the tambourine on beat 3 of each set.

Tambourine

hit   hit shake hit   hit shake hit   hit shake
elbow

Play the tambourine pattern along with the recording.

 *The Unhappy Cuckoo*

You have played the rhythm of a dance called the *mazurka.*

DANCE

To dance a mazurka, walk forward on the first two beats of the measure and hop on the third beat. Begin with either foot. Make your movements match the meter of the music.

Mazurka
step   step step hop step step hop step step hop

Try the mazurka step, stepping sideways to the left or to the right.

DANCE IN TWOS: POLKA

Play beats in sets of two on the maracas. Make the first beat
of each set stronger than the others.

Now play this pattern along with the recording.

Emilia Polka

You have played the rhythm of a dance called the *polka.*

Dance the polka step throughout section B of "In Bahia Town."

step   slide   step   hop step   slide   step   hop

In Bahia Town
FOLK SONG FROM BRAZIL   ENGLISH WORDS BY VERNE MUÑOZ

MELODY FROM FOLK SONGS AND DANCES OF THE AMERICAS, PUBLISHED BY THE GENERAL SECRETARIAT OF THE ORGANIZATION OF AMERICAN STATES.

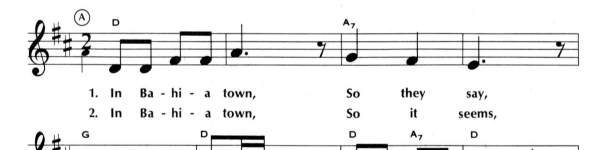

1. In Ba - hi - a town,   So   they   say,
2. In Ba - hi - a town,   So   it   seems,

They sell co - co - nuts for a pen - ny In the mar - ket place.
You can buy a sew - ing ma-chine That stitch - es like a dream.

In Ba - hi - a town,   So   they   say,
In Ba - hi - a town,   So   it   seems,

80

They sell fish that's bet - ter than an - y You will ev - er taste.
You can buy a lamp made of glass In shades of blue and green.

La la la la la la la la la, La la la la la la la,

La la la la la la la la la, La la la la la la.

WHAT DO YOU HEAR? 5: Meter

Can you hear meter in this music?

Listen to the recording to discover whether the meter is in 2 or in 3.

1 *METER IN 2*	*METER IN 3*	Stravinsky: *Suite No. 2 for Small Orchestra,* "Valse"
2 *METER IN 2*	*METER IN 3*	Bizet: *Carmen Suite,* "March of the Street Urchins"
3 *METER IN 2*	*METER IN 3*	Gershwin: *An American in Paris*
4 *METER IN 2*	*METER IN 3*	Dvořák: *Slavonic Dances,* Op. 46, No. 6
5 *METER IN 2*	*METER IN 3*	Scruggs: *String Bender*
6 *METER IN 2*	*METER IN 3*	Saint-Saëns: *Carnival of the Animals,* "The Elephant"

Modern Styles

STYLE IN PAINTING

These are two modern paintings. What makes
them different in style? How are they alike?

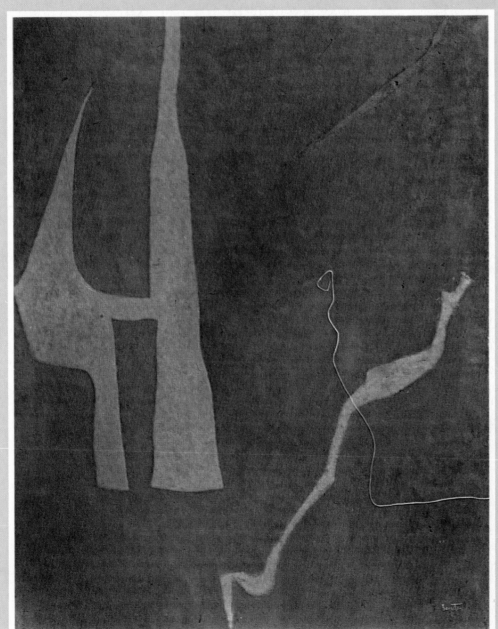

THE SOLOMON R. GUGGENHEIM MUSEUM COLLECTION; WILLIAM BAZIOTES; DUSK, 1958.

83

STYLE IN MUSIC

These are two modern pieces of music. As you listen,
follow the words that show what makes these pieces
different in style. How are these pieces alike?

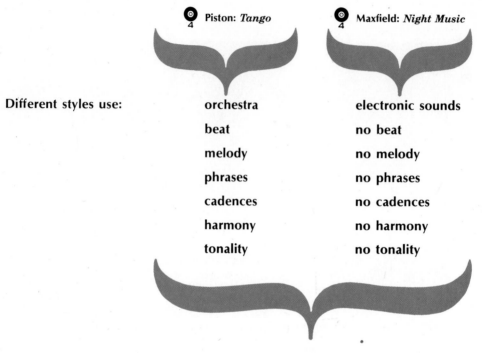

    Piston: *Tango*   **Maxfield:** *Night Music*

Different styles use:

orchestra	electronic sounds
beat	no beat
melody	no melody
phrases	no phrases
cadences	no cadences
harmony	no harmony
tonality	no tonality

Both these pieces use:

high and low sounds

short and long sounds

repeated sounds

steps and leaps

several sounds together

upward and downward direction

Copland: *Celebration*

Babbitt: *Ensembles for Synthesizer*

Modern painting and modern music have many styles.
Some things are different in different styles, but some things
are the same no matter what the style.

STYLE IN POETRY

GERANIUM

Mary Ellen Solt

The words appearing in the figure include:

SUMMER
TIMES
GOD'S
EXIT
SUMMER
SILENCE
MEASURES
RESOUNDS
UMBELAR
INTERPRETS
ANSWERS
RED
NO ONE
A CAPELLA
SEEN
EACH

Dynamics: *Loud/Soft*

These three pictures show something about volume. Which picture shows that the sound is loud? What do the other pictures show?

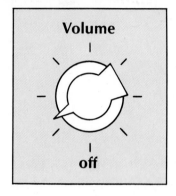

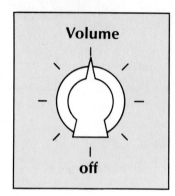

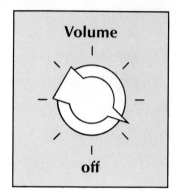

"Louds" and "softs" are called *dynamics.* Use dynamics when you recite a poem.

TOM AND JOE

Tom loves to be heard;
Joe not at all.
Boom!
Can you hear Joe's small
voice? No? It seems to have died!
Boom!
You can hear *that*, though?
Yes? Well, *I told you so!*
I imply—I've implied;
You infer—you've inferred
that I'm *not* on Tom's side,
nor on Joe's. My one word
is: *Don't* be a Tom
who explodes like a bomb.
And oh, yes: on the other
hand, *Don't* be a Joe!

David McCord

Use dynamics when you sing a song. *The Hi-Dee-Ho Man*

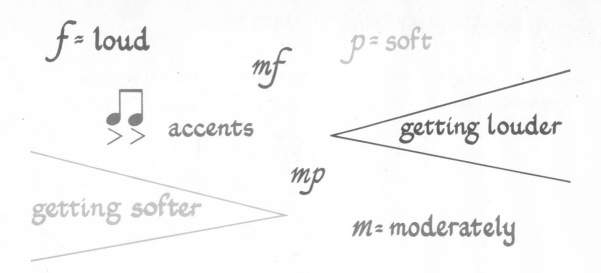

f = loud

mf

p = soft

accents

getting louder

getting softer

mp

m = moderately

There are two dynamic marks in the music that tell you how to sing this song. Can you find them?

Up the Street the Band Is Marching Down

WORDS AND MUSIC BY LUIGI ZANINELLI

I f

Up   the street   the band   is   march-ing   down,

II

Hear   the   fi - fers shrill,   See   the   drum-mer's skill,

III

Tramp,   tramp,   tramp,   round   the town,   round   the town;

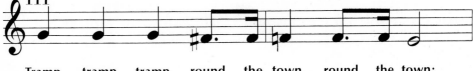

If   the trum-pets make an   er - ror,   See their fac - es pale with ter - ror.

AFRICAN RHYTHM COMPLEX

Say the numbers in each line below. Clap each time you say a large-size number.

$$1 \quad {}_2 \quad 3 \quad {}_4 \quad 5 \quad 6 \quad {}_7 \quad 8 \quad {}_9 \quad 10 \quad {}_{11} \quad 12$$

$$1 \quad {}_2 \quad {}_3 \quad 4 \quad {}_5 \quad {}_6 \quad 7 \quad {}_8 \quad {}_9 \quad 10 \quad {}_{11} \quad {}_{12}$$

$$1 \quad {}_2 \quad 3 \quad 4 \quad 5 \quad 6 \quad 7 \quad 8 \quad 9 \quad 10 \quad 11 \quad 12$$

$$1 \, 2 \, 3 \, 4 \quad {}_5 \quad {}_6 \quad 7 \, 8 \, 9 \, 10 \quad {}_{11} \quad {}_{12}$$

Now, instead of clapping the large-size numbers, play them on a percussion instrument.

Try different dynamics and tempos and create your own African rhythm complex.

As you listen to the recording of *African Rhythm Complex*, follow the notation on page 89.

◎ *African Rhythm Complex*
4

88

Here is the notation for the rhythms you clapped.

Bell 1

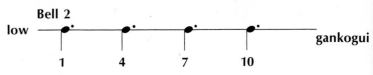

high
low

1   3   5   6   8   10   12

Bell 2

low

1   4   7   10

gankogui

Rattle

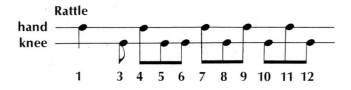

hand
knee

1   3   4   5   6   7   8   9   10   11   12

High Drum

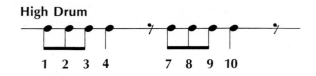

1   2   3   4   7   8   9   10

axatse

CHALLENGE

Choose an instrument—bell, rattle, or drum. Then play one of the rhythms along with the recording.

kagan

ACCENTS

Play these patterns on a tambourine when you sing "Dundai."

Which pattern has accents? Will you play the section B pattern

loud, or soft? Why?

Dundai

HEBREW FOLK SONG   ENGLISH WORDS BY HAROLD AKS

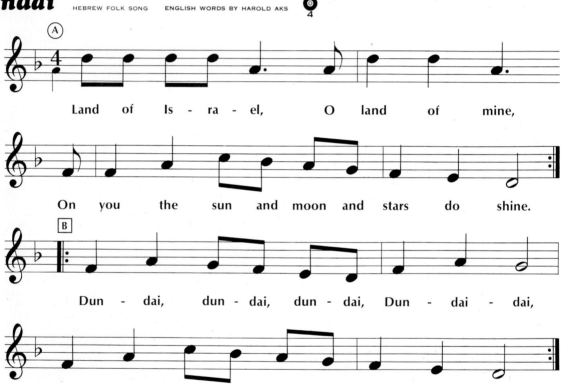

Land of Is - ra - el, O land of mine,

On you the sun and moon and stars do shine.

Dun - dai, dun - dai, dun - dai, Dun - dai - dai,

Dun - dai, dun - dai, dun - dai, Dun - dai - dai.

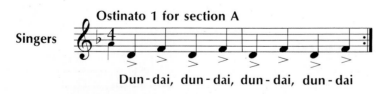

Singers

Ostinato 1 for section A

Dun - dai, dun - dai, dun - dai, dun - dai

Recorder
or
Bells

Ostinato 2 for section B

DYNAMIC PLAN FOR "GING GONG GOOLI"

Play these tambourine parts to accompany "Ging Gong Gooli," page 18.
The letters and symbols will tell you how to use dynamics.

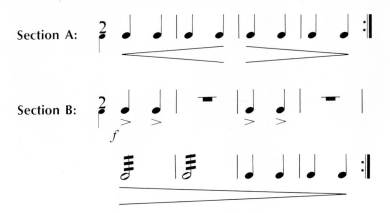

CALL CHART 4: Dynamics

How are dynamics used in this music? Listen to the recording.
As each number is called, look at the chart. It will help you
hear the changes in dynamics.

Ward: *America, the Beautiful*

1	MF	(MODERATELY LOUD)
2	P	(SOFT)
3	◁	(GETTING LOUDER)
4	P	(SOFT)
5	◁	(GETTING LOUDER)
6	P	(SOFT)
7	MF	(MODERATELY LOUD)
8	◁	(GETTING LOUDER)

Remember Me

BLACK SPIRITUAL

4

VERSE

1. When chill - y winds blow from the North,___ I've got to go;
2. I've got a home in glo - ry land,___ out - shines the sun;

When chill - y winds blow from the North,___ I've got to go;
I've got a home in glo - ry land___ out - shines the sun;

When chill - y winds blow from the North,___ I've got to go;
I've got a home in glo - ry land___ out - shines the sun;

A - way up be - yond ___ the moon.

REFRAIN

(optional harmony part)

Do, Lord, O do, Lord, O do re - mem - ber me;

Do, Lord, O do, Lord, O do re - mem - ber me;

Do, Lord, O do, Lord, O do re - mem - ber me;

A - way up be - yond ___ the moon.

92

WHAT DO YOU HEAR?   6: Dynamics ◉

Listen to these pieces. Each time a number is called,
decide which of the three answers is correct.
Choose the answer that best describes what is happening in the music.

1	PIANO	FORTE	<>	1	PIANO	FORTE	<>
2	PIANO	FORTE	<>	2	PIANO	FORTE	<>
3	PIANO	FORTE	<>	3	PIANO	FORTE	<>

Mendelssohn: *Symphony No. 5*, Mvt. 2   Bizet: *Scènes Bohémiennes*, No. 3

WHAT DO YOU HEAR?   7: Dynamics ◉

Listen to these pieces. Choose the answers that best describe
the dynamics. Is the music all soft? All loud? Soft and loud?

Do you hear accents? If you do, choose the word *accents*.
If you do not, choose the words *no accents*.

1	ALL P	ALL F	P AND F	ACCENTS	NO ACCENTS

Stockhausen: *Klavierstück*

2	ALL P	ALL F	P AND F	ACCENTS	NO ACCENTS

Ives: *The Pond*

3	ALL P	ALL F	P AND F	ACCENTS	NO ACCENTS

Olantunji: *Jin-Go-Lo-Ba*

4	ALL P	ALL F	P AND F	ACCENTS	NO ACCENTS

Alkan: *Les Diablotins*

Form

Find shapes and colors that repeat or contrast in the
photograph on the opposite page.

Shapes and letters can show form in music. Which shapes and
letters show the form of songs you know?

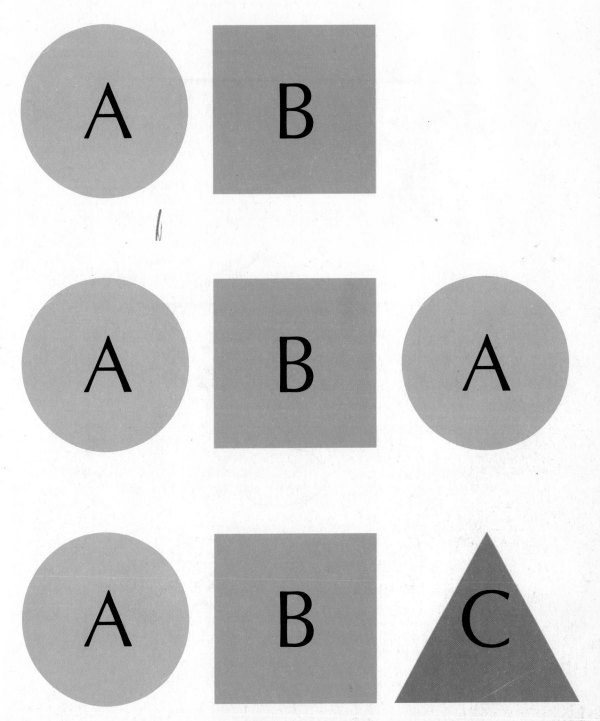

$\boxed{A}$ $\boxed{B}$ FORM

Sands Get into Your Shoes

WORDS AND MUSIC BY ARTHUR CARTER

USED BY PERMISSION.

1. You have -n't lived___ in the sum - mer - time___
2. The sun comes beat - ing down on your head,___

Un - til you've gone___ to the beach,___
The dust gets in - to your eyes,___

And tast - ed ice - cream: the lem - on lime,___
Your feet they hurt,___ but the thing you dread's___

Ba - na - na, wal - nut and peach.
The mos - qui - toes___ and the flies.

(optional harmony part)

And sands, and sands, and sands get in - to your o - pen shoes,

And sands, and sands, and sands get in - to your shoes.

3. You leave your things by the waterside,
   And then somehow you forget
   To move them back from the rising tide—
   Your towels and blanket get wet.
   And sands . . .

HOW TO CONTRAST SECTIONS

Show a contrast between the two sections of "Sands Get into Your Shoes" by playing instruments.

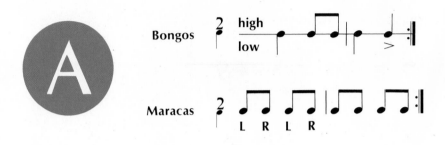

Add a different Autoharp part for each section. Make up your own patterns of long and short strums.

Show a contrast between the two sections of *Flop-Eared Mule* by moving. Use one movement pattern for the A sections; use a different pattern for the B sections.

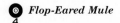

Flop-Eared Mule
4

Ⓐ Ⓑ Ⓐ FORM

The sign in the color box tells you to go back to the beginning
of the song and sing section A again.

To show repetition and contrast, move during the A sections;
play any percussion instrument during section B.

Run, Run, Run

WORDS AND MUSIC BY CHRIS DEDRICK

© 1972 ALMITRA MUSIC COMPANY, INC.

mf
Run, run, run ___ through the sun-light, Run, run, run ___ through the snow.

Fine
Run, run, run, ___ don't be up-tight, Run, run, run, ___ Free-dom, go. ___

mp
If you're glad that you can use your legs, they're free;

If you're glad that you can use your eyes to see,

If you're glad the world has trea-sures you can find,

D.C. al Fine
Go and run so fast your cares are left be-hind.

"RUN, RUN, RUN" FOR RECORDER

Play this part on the recorder (or bells) when it comes in the song. It uses G and A—notes you have played before.

Recorder (or Bells) 1

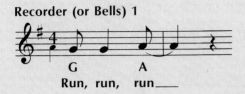

G   A

Run, run, run___

TWO NEW NOTES

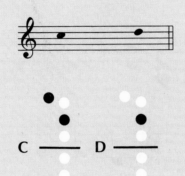

C ——— D ———

Now try playing this part during section A.

Recorder (or Bells) 2

A   B D   C   B

(Run, run, run)   through the sun-light,   (Run, run, run)   through the snow.

A   D B   C B G

(Run, run, run,) don't be up-tight, (Run, run, run,) Free-dom, go.___

CHALLENGE: Review the recorder notes on pages 27 and 59. Then try playing the whole song.

SHOW THE FORM

The words and music of this lively song will make you want to get up and move!

Start off with one movement pattern. When you hear a new section, change your movement. How will you move if a section is repeated?

Don't Count Your Chickens

WORDS AND MUSIC BY CARMINO RAVOSA

© 1971 Carmino Ravosa

Don't count your chick-ens be - fore they hatch, Be - fore they hatch,

be - fore they hatch. Don't count your chick-ens be - fore they hatch,

Be - fore they hatch, (clap clap) they hatch!

Don't you plan a - bout to-mor-row, 'cause to-mor-row does-n't come un - til to -

mor - row; Have a lot - ta fun to-day be-cause to -

mor-row may just bring a lot-ta sor - row. Don't you sor - row.

Don't count your chick-ens be - fore they hatch, Be - fore they hatch,

be - fore they hatch. Don't count your chick-ens be - fore they hatch,

Be - fore they hatch, (*clap clap*) they hatch!

As you sing the song, take turns adding a cluster of tones on the words *they hatch*. To play a cluster, strike a group of bells with the edge of a small wooden ruler. Or play a group of piano keys with your knuckles.

Will you play a cluster of high tones, or low tones?

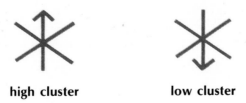

high cluster   low cluster

Ask two friends to help you play clusters of tones on recorders. One recorder plays G, another plays A, the third plays B—all at the same time.

they   hatch

CALL CHART 5: Form 🎵
₅

Can you hear form in music? Listen to the recording to discover the form of these pieces? When number 1 is called, you are hearing section A. When you hear another number, the music will be either a repetition of section A, or a contrast. Follow the chart to help you hear what is happening in the music.

---

1   *A*

2   *CONTRAST*   *B*   *Notebook for Anna Magdalena Bach,* "Minuet"

---

1   *A*

2   *CONTRAST*   *B*

3   *REPETITION*   *A*   **Bichel:** *Happy Moments*

---

1   *A*

2   *REPETITION*   *A*

3   *CONTRAST*   *B*

4   *REPETITION*   *A*   *Notebook for Anna Magdalena Bach,* "Musette"

THREE DIFFERENT SECTIONS

Create a sound piece that has three different sections. Use the tone colors and rhythm patterns shown below.

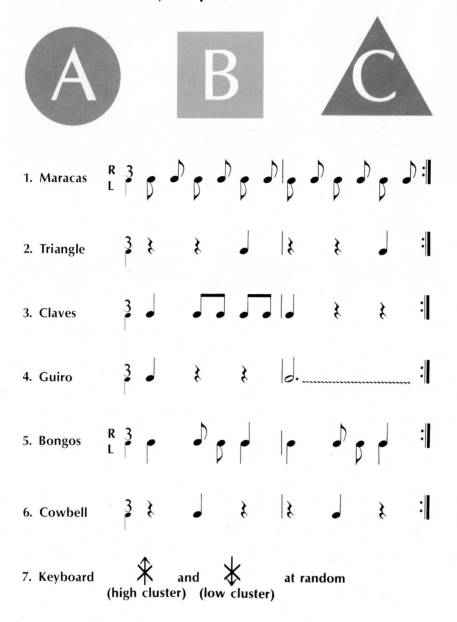

7. Keyboard ☧ (high cluster) and ☒ (low cluster) at random

Ways to contrast sections:

    1. Different tone colors

    2. Different rhythm patterns

    3. Different dynamics—p, mf, f, < >

    4. Different tempos

 FORM

The African words of this song mean "We are the burning fire; we burn; we burn!"

Use a strong singing voice, but don't shout.

Tina, Singu   FOLK SONG FROM AFRICA

FROM CHANSONS DE NOTRE CHALET. COURTESY OF WORLD AROUND SONGS. BURNSVILLE, N.C.

CHALLENGE: How do the tones move in each of the three sections?

- Section ? has a tone that repeats many times.

- Section ? has sets of repeated tones that move upward.

- Section ? has tones that leap as well as tones that move by step.

CALL CHART 6: Form 🔘

Repetition and contrast can be used in many ways to give music form. Listen to the recording to discover how contrast is used to make version 2 of this piece different from version 1.

Following the chart will help you to hear what is going on in the music.

Kingsley: *Electronic Rondo,* Versions 1 and 2

Version 1

1		A
2	FIRST CONTRAST	B
3	REPETITION	A
4	FIRST CONTRAST	B
5	REPETITION	A

Version 2

1		A
2	FIRST CONTRAST	B
3	REPETITION	A
4	SECOND CONTRAST	C
5	REPETITION	A

Guava Berry Song

CHRISTMAS SONG FROM THE VIRGIN ISLANDS   ENGLISH WORDS BY JOAN GILBERT VAN POZNAK

FROM UNICEF BOOK OF CHILDREN'S SONGS, COMPILED AND WITH PHOTOGRAPHS BY WILLIAM I. KAUFMAN, COPYRIGHT 1970 BY WILLIAM I. KAUFMAN, PUBLISHED BY STACKPOLE BOOKS.

Come let us be joy-ful, and min-gle our song,

And hail the sweet joys which this day brings a - long.

We join our glad voic - es in one hymn of praise

To ___ Him ___ who has kept us, and ___ length-ened our days.

A mer - ry Christ-mas to you all, A mer - ry Christ-mas to you all,

SOUND PIECE 5: Running Sound Shapes

DAVID S. WALKER

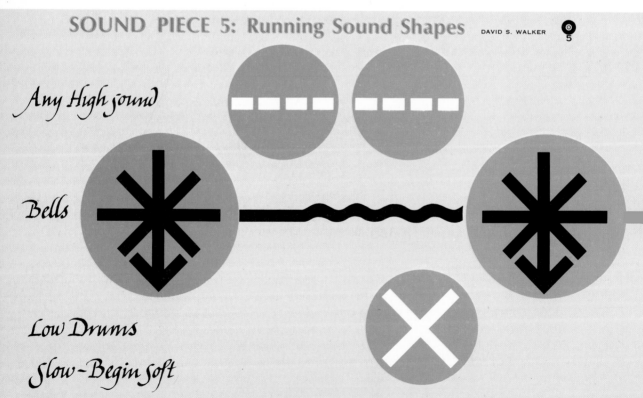

Any High sound

Bells

Low Drums

Slow-Begin soft

A mer-ry Christ-mas, A mer-ry Christ-mas, A mer-ry Christ-mas to you all!

Good morn-in', good morn-in', We wish you a mer-ry Christ-mas,

Good morn-in', good morn-in', We wish you a mer-ry Christ-mas,

Good morn-in', good morn-in', We've come for the gua-va ber-ry,

Good morn-in', good morn-in', Oh put it on the ta-ble.

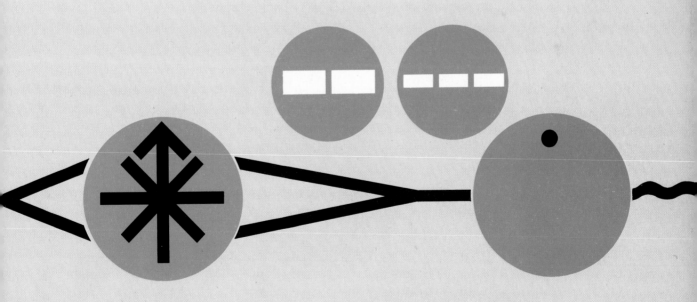

USING SYMBOLS

The music at the bottom of pages 106–111 in your book is written using the shapes ● and ■. This is to show that the piece has two sections. Where does section B begin?

Here is what the symbols in *Sound Piece 5* stand for.

LEGEND

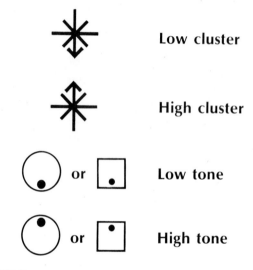

Low cluster

High cluster

Low tone

High tone

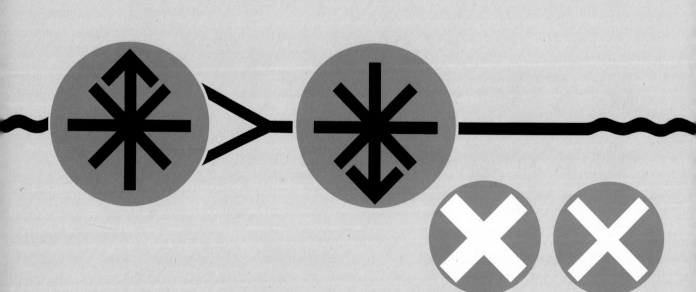

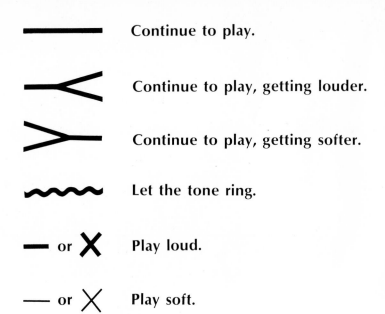 Continue to play.

Continue to play, getting louder.

Continue to play, getting softer.

Let the tone ring.

— or ✕ Play loud.

— or ✕ Play soft.

Now practice section A. While you play the bells, have one friend play the drum part, another the top part.

Another time, try section B. When your ensemble is ready to play *Sound Piece 5,* perform for the class.

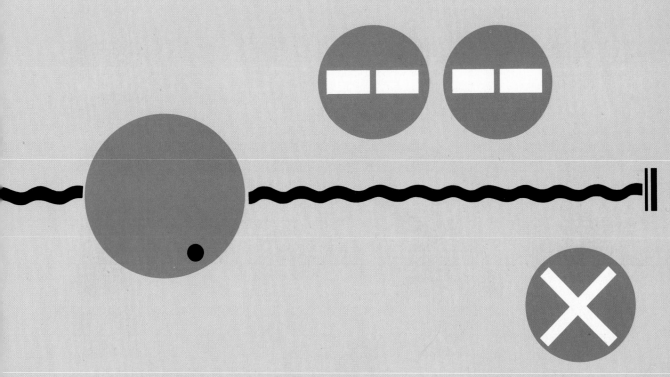

Can you hear repetition and contrast in these pieces?

When number "one" is called, you will hear the musical ideas
in section A. As the other numbers are called, decide whether
the music is a repetition of A, a first contrast of A (B), or a
second contrast of A (C).

---

1   A
2   A B   Purcell: *Fanfare*

---

1   A
2   A B
3   A B C   *Guava Berry Song*

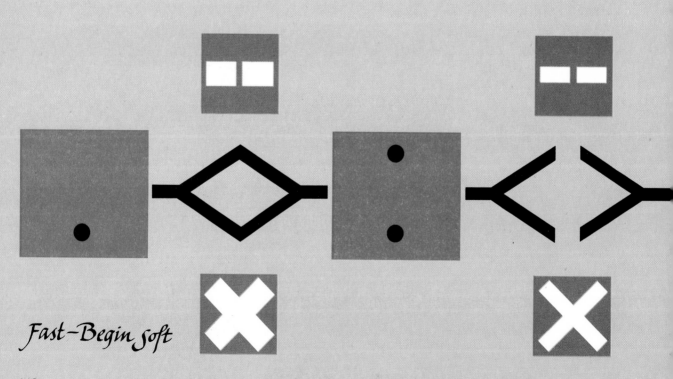

Fast–Begin soft

1	*A*		
2	*A*	*B*	
3	*A*	*B*	*C*

Britten: *Scherzo* (1955)

1	*A*		
2	*A*	*B*	
3	*A*	*B*	*C*
4	*A*	*B*	*C*

Tchaikovsky: ***Nutcracker Suite,*** "Trepak"

1	*A*		
2	*A*	*B*	
3	*A*	*B*	*C*
4	*A*	*B*	*C*
5	*A*	*B*	*C*

Kingsley: ***Electronic Rondo,*** Version 2

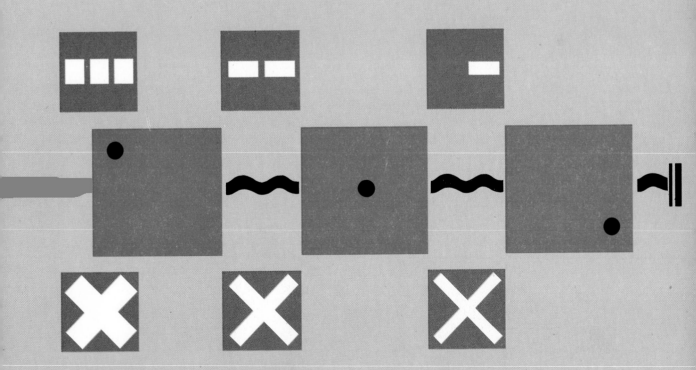

Style

Everything is
made of parts.

Put the parts together
and you get a "whole."

What do these numbers and colors add up to?

$$11 + 9 + 8 + 2 = 30$$

When you add the numbers, the answer is 30.

When yellow and blue are combined, the result is green.

On the recording *Combining Sounds,* you will hear the following sounds combined in two ways.

1. *LOW, SOFT SOUNDS*

2. *HIGH, LOUD SOUNDS*

3. *LONG AND SHORT SOUNDS*

4. *SOUNDS MOVING IN BOTH UPWARD AND DOWNWARD DIRECTIONS*

Do the combined sounds result in the same general sound each time?

Combining Sounds

When certain numbers or colors are combined, the result is always the same.

When certain qualities of sounds are used, the combinations of sounds may result in the same style, or in different styles.

1. **Listen to this piece.**

   It uses many musical qualities—tone color, texture, etc.

   Decide what you hear for each quality listed below.

Marcello: *Sonata in F*, Movement 4

Tone Color	TRUMPET SAXOPHONE	FLUTE PIANO
Texture	MELODY WITH HARMONY	MELODY ALONE
Form	NO REPETITION AND CONTRAST	REPETITION AND CONTRAST
Direction	UPWARD DOWNWARD	BOTH UPWARD AND DOWNWARD
Duration	LONG SHORT	BOTH LONG AND SHORT
Dynamics	SOFT LOUD	BOTH SOFT AND LOUD
Phrases	SHORT LONG	BOTH SHORT AND LONG

2. Now listen to another piece.

It uses the same musical qualities as the first piece.

What do you hear for each quality in this music?

Caplet: *Petite Valse*

Tone Color	TRUMPET	FLUTE
	SAXOPHONE	PIANO

Texture	MELODY WITH	MELODY
	HARMONY	ALONE

Form	NO REPETITION	REPETITION AND
	AND CONTRAST	CONTRAST

Direction	UPWARD	BOTH UPWARD
	DOWNWARD	AND DOWNWARD

Duration	LONG	BOTH LONG
	SHORT	AND SHORT

Dynamics	SOFT	BOTH SOFT
	LOUD	AND LOUD

Phrases	SHORT	BOTH SHORT
	LONG	AND LONG

Register—Range

Listen to the recording. What voices and instruments are producing

- high sounds?
- low sounds?
- sounds in the middle?

🔘 *Shoo-Be-de-doop*
5

In music, highness or lowness of sound is called *register*.

LOW

HIGH

MIDDLE

117

LOW ECHO OR HIGH ECHO?

Will you sing the echo part in a high register, or a low register?

Island Hopping

FOLK SONG FROM GREECE   ENGLISH WORDS BY MARIA JORDAN

1. Bags are packed and all is rea - dy, can't wait ___ to

start; (can't wait ___ to start;) Boat is board-ing at the jet - ty,

soon we'll ___ de - part. (soon we'll ___ de - part.)

B G (optional harmony part)
Is - land hop - ping we ___ are ___ go - ing,

Sea is calm, a soft ___ wind's ___ blow - ing,

We can feel ex - cite - ment ___ grow - ing

in ev - 'ry heart, ___ *Ahs-toh kah-loh,* ___ In ev - 'ry ___ heart.

2. Parents with their sons and daughters planned for this day;
Now the boat glides 'cross the waters, we're on our way.
Grecian islands lie before us—
Hydra, Spetsai, lovely Poros
Beckon us as, in a chorus, "Come," they all say, *Ahstoh kahloh*,
"Come," they all say.

Play the echo in section A in a high register or in a low register.

Bells

E C♯ B A D

Arrange the high bells like this.

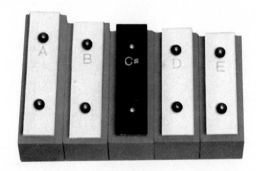

Arrange the low bells like this.

119

LOW—HIGH—MIDDLE

You can accompany "Rally Song" with one Autoharp chord—
D min. Vary the sound of the accompaniment by strumming the
low strings, then the high strings. Use this pattern or make up
one of your own.

Rally Song

ROUND FROM THE BALKANS

FROM THE 1960 REVISED VERSION OF THE DITTY BAG BY JANET TOBITT. USED BY PERMISSION.

Mi ha - bi lu - lu be-shem-bel. Mi ha - bi lu - lu be-shem-bel.

Mi ha - bi lu - lu be-shem-bel. Mi ha - bi lu - lu be-shem-bel.

Now play an Autoharp accompaniment using only the strings in
the middle register.

When you accompany "Rally Song" another time, strum in a
low, middle, or high register. You decide.

Experiment to find two percussion instruments—one with a
high sound, one with a low sound.

When "Rally Song" is sung as a round, accompany group I with
high sounds and group II with low sounds. Play the rhythm of
the words.

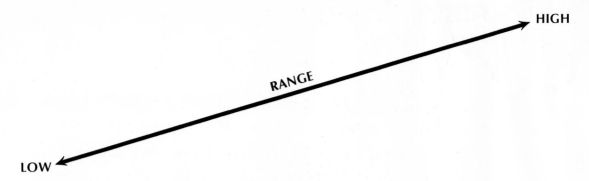

RANGE HIGH

LOW

Take turns accompanying "Rally Song" by playing one of these ostinato patterns on recorder or bells.

Which pattern has the widest range? To find out, count the notes from the lowest to the highest.

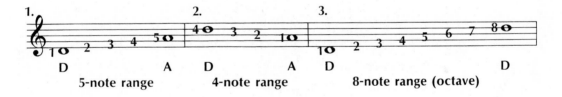

1.
D   A
5-note range

2.
D   A
4-note range

3.
D   D
8-note range (octave)

Look at the score of "Rally Song" on page 120. Does the melody have a 4-note range? A 5-note range? An octave range?

What is the range of this countermelody for "Rally Song"?

Recorder or Bells

I

D   A   D

II

D   A   D

Hold On

AMERICAN FOLK SONG

How would you sing strong words like *hold on*?

(A) VERSE

D MIN.

1. When you plow, don't lose your track,___
2. If you want to get to heaven, I'll tell you how,___

D MIN.   D MIN.   A₇   D MIN.

Can't plow straight and keep a - look - in' back.___
Keep your hand___ right___ on___ that plow.___

D MIN.

Keep your hand on___ that plow,___
Keep your hand on___ that plow,___

D MIN.   G MIN.   D MIN.   (B) REFRAIN A₇   D MIN.

Hold on, hold on, hold on.
Hold on, hold on, hold on.   Hold on, hold on,

D MIN.   A₇   D MIN.

Bet - ter keep your hand right on___ that plow,___

D MIN.   G MIN.   D MIN.

Hold on, hold on, hold on.

3. Keep on plowin' and don't you tire,
   Ev'ry row goes higher and higher.
   Keep your hand on that plow,
   Hold on, hold on, hold on. *Refrain*

4. If that plow stays in your hand,
   Head you straight for the promised land.
   Keep your hand on that plow,
   Hold on, hold on, hold on. *Refrain*

Old Blue

SOUTHERN MOUNTAIN SONG

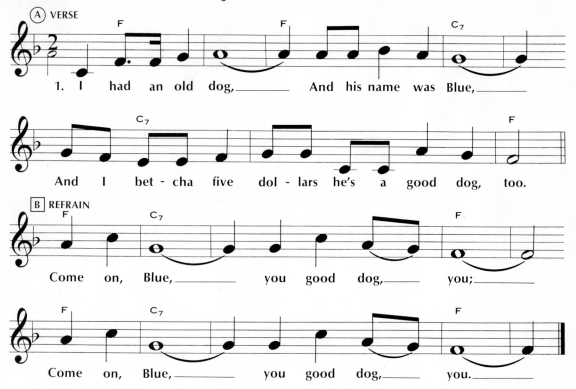

A VERSE

1. I had an old dog,_____ And his name was Blue,_____

And I bet-cha five dol-lars he's a good dog, too.

B REFRAIN

Come on, Blue,_____ you good dog,_____ you;_____

Come on, Blue,_____ you good dog,_____ you._____

2. I grabbed my axe and I tooted my horn,

   Gonna git me a 'possum in the new-ground corn. *Refrain*

3. Chased that ol' 'possum up a 'simmon tree,

   Blue looked at the 'possum, 'possum looked at me. *Refrain*

4. Blue grinned at me, I grinned at him,

   I shook out the 'possum, Blue took him in. *Refrain*

5. Baked that 'possum all good and brown,

   And I laid them sweet potatoes 'round and 'round. *Refrain*

6. Well, old Blue died, and he died so hard,

   That he shook the ground in my back yard. *Refrain*

7. I dug his grave with a silver spade,

   I let him down with a golden chain. *Refrain*

8. When I get to heaven, first thing I'll do,

   Grab me a horn and blow for old Blue. *Refrain*

Can you hear how a modern composer has given a new sound to an old familiar song?

Stravinsky: *Greeting Prelude*

SOUND PIECE 6: Music Boxes   JOYCE BOGUSKY-REIMER   © 1980 JOYCE BOGUSKY-REIMER

Choose an instrument that makes both high and low sounds.

Then practice the events in the boxes below.

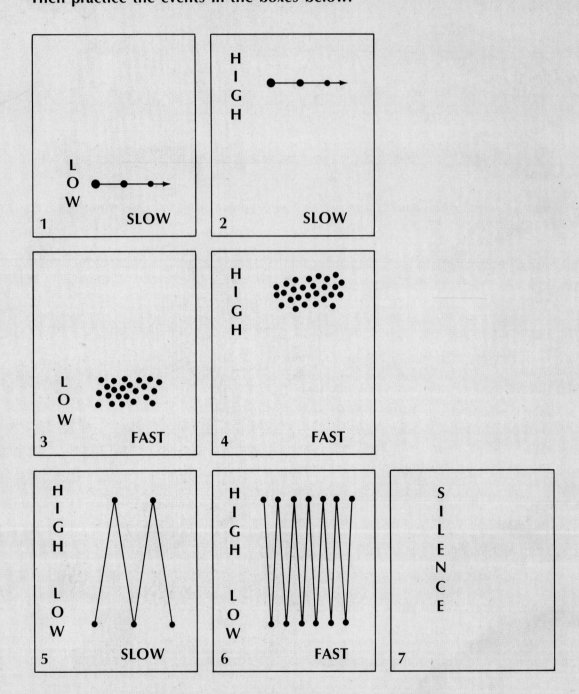

Now play the boxes in an order that gives the piece form.

You may start with any box, repeat some boxes, or omit some boxes.

AN AFRICAN PERFORMER

On the recording, an African performer of the Kpelle tribe plays the triangular framed zither. Listen for the different registers in the music—low, middle, high.

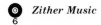 *Zither Music*

LOW/HIGH

Find the lowest note and the highest note in this song.

What is the range?

Song of the Angel

MENNONITE MELODY © 1966 BY LAWSON GOULD MUSIC PUBLISHERS, INC. USED BY PERMISSION

1. Fear not, fear not, good shep - herds all,

Let faith your fear de - stroy;

For lo, this night I bring to you

Good ti - dings of great joy,

Good ti - dings of great joy.

2. Awake your ears and hark to me,
   To hear the glorious Word:
   For unto you is born this day
   A Saviour, Christ the Lord,
   A Saviour, Christ the Lord.

3. You'll find the Babe in Bethlehem,
   Born of the Mary maid;
   All wrapped in swaddling clothes is He,
   And in a manger laid,
   And in a manger laid.

4. So join us now with one accord
   To sing this wondrous birth:
   Give praise to God, our heav'nly King,
   And peace to men on earth,
   And peace to men on earth.

126

HIGH/LOW

As you sing about the seasons of the year, notice which phrase you sing in a high register; in a low register.

The Seasons of the Year

WORDS AND MUSIC BY PETER CROSSLEY-HOLLAND

I Rain and sun and frost and snow;

II Spring and Sum - mer, Au - tumn, Win - ter,

III Round and round the sea - sons go.

Which has a wider range, this ostinato, or the melody of "The Seasons of the Year"?

Ostinato—Recorder or Bells

G A B A

Look at the notes in the color box. They are the lowest and highest notes in the melody. What is the range?

For Health and Strength

OLD ENGLISH ROUND

I F For health and II strength and dai - ly food We III praise Thy name, O Lord.

Two Little Pieces, No. 1

ANTON BRUCKNER

FROM 44 ORIGINAL PIANO DUETS AS EDITED BY WALTER ECKARD. © 1962 THEODORE PRESSER COMPANY. USED BY PERMISSION.

WHAT DO YOU HEAR?   10: Register ◉

Listen to this piece. Each time a number is called, choose the answer (or answers) that best describes the register.

Haydn: *Chorale St. Antonie*

1	HIGH REGISTER	MIDDLE REGISTER	LOW REGISTER
2	HIGH REGISTER	MIDDLE REGISTER	LOW REGISTER
3	HIGH REGISTER	MIDDLE REGISTER	LOW REGISTER
4	HIGH REGISTER	MIDDLE REGISTER	LOW REGISTER

WHAT DO YOU HEAR?   11: Range ◉

Listen to these pieces. Each time a number is called, choose the answer that best describes the range.

1	NARROW RANGE	WIDE RANGE	Webern: *Variations for Orchestra*
2	NARROW RANGE	WIDE RANGE	*Gregorian Chant*
3	NARROW RANGE	WIDE RANGE	Tchaikovsky: *The Sleeping Beauty*
4	NARROW RANGE	WIDE RANGE	*Ai a la o Pele*

The Arts: Repetition With Variety and Contrast

Follow the rhythm patterns below as you listen to the recording. They will help you hear what is going on in the upper parts of the music.

Eddleman: *For Health and Strength* (*Ground with Variations*)

1. Ground (melody) alone

Can you see repetition as well as variety and contrast in the photograph on page 130 and in the painting above?

YOU'RE ON YOUR OWN

Use the melody of "Rally Song" as a ground. Add variety and contrast by performing one of the parts on p. 133. Use the recording of the ground while you practice your part.

 *Rally Song* (Ground)

When you and your classmates are ready, follow this arrangement as the ground repeats on the recording.

1. ground alone

2. ground, bells, and Autoharp

3.
4. } *ground, round, and tambourine*

5.
6. } *ground, bells, Autoharp, round, and tambourine*

Ground ("Rally Song") FROM THE 1960 REVISED VERSION OF THE DITTY BAG BY JANET TOBITT. USED BY PERMISSION.

Bells or Recorder

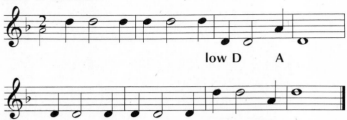

low D   A

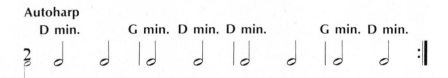

Autoharp

D min.   G min. D min. D min.   G min. D min.

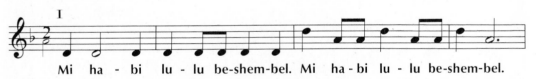

Round ("Rally Song")

I

Mi ha - bi lu - lu be-shem-bel. Mi ha - bi lu - lu be-shem-bel.

II

Mi ha - bi lu - lu be-shem-bel. Mi ha - bi lu - lu be-shem-bel.

Tambourine   **(shake)**

Rhythm Patterns

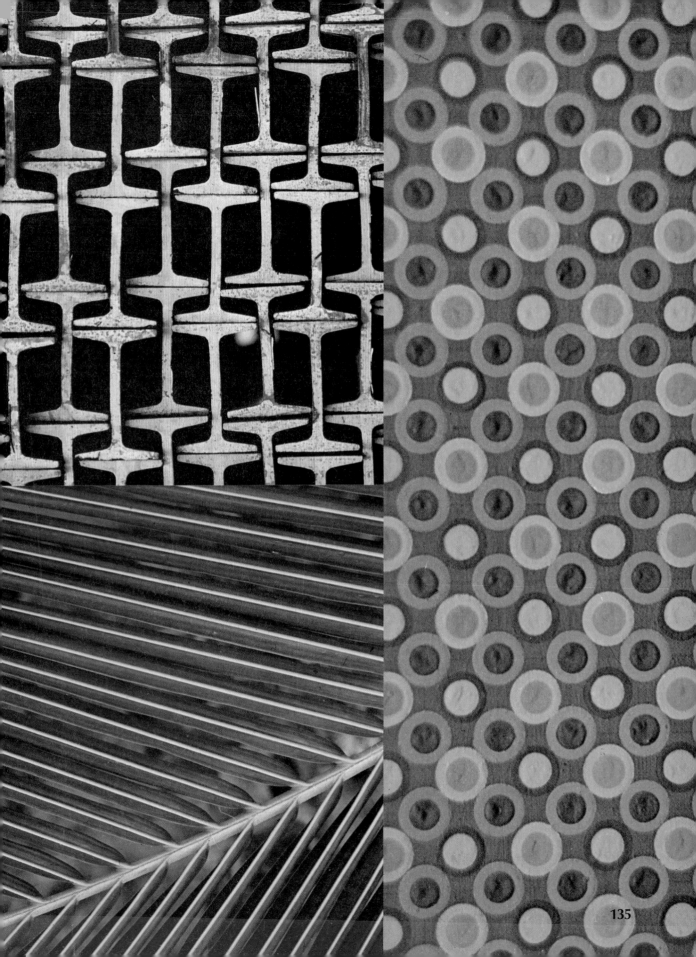

135

LONG SOUNDS, SHORT SOUNDS

Follow the voice parts as you listen to the recording of
"Old Texas." Notice that one part sings short sounds while
the other sings long ones.

As others sing the long sounds in the melody,
take turns strumming a rhythm pattern on the
Autoharp. The score will tell you when to play
the F chord and when to play the C_7 chord.

Old Texas   OKLAHOMA COWBOY SONG

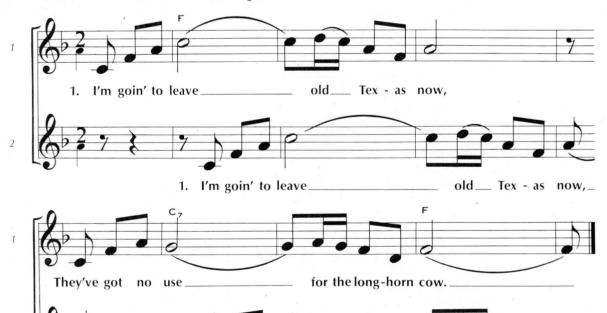

1. I'm goin' to leave _____ old __ Tex - as now,

1. I'm goin' to leave _____ old __ Tex - as now, __

They've got no use _____ for the long-horn cow. __

___ They've got no use _____ for the long-horn cow.

2. They've plowed and fenced my cattle range,
   And the people there are all so strange.

3. I'll take my horse, I'll take my rope,
   And hit the trail upon a lope.

4. Say *adios* to the Alamo
   And turn my head toward Mexico.

CALL CHART 7: Rhythm Patterns ◉₆

Listen to this piece. Each time a number is called, decide whether you are hearing long sounds or short sounds. Look at the chart to check your answers.

Schumann: *Fantasiestücke*, Op. 12, No. 6, "Fable"

---

1   *LONG*

---

2   *SHORT*

---

3   *LONG*

---

4   *SHORT*

---

5   *SHORT*

---

6   *LONG*

---

7   *LONG*

LONG AND SHORT TOGETHER

There are many ways to combine long and short sounds and long and short silences to make rhythm patterns.

Can you hear long and short sounds played at the same time in this music? Strings play the long sounds. Brass instruments play the short sounds.

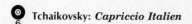 ◉₆ Tchaikovsky: *Capriccio Italien*

TABLA—DRUMS OF INDIA

Tabla are among the most popular drums of India.

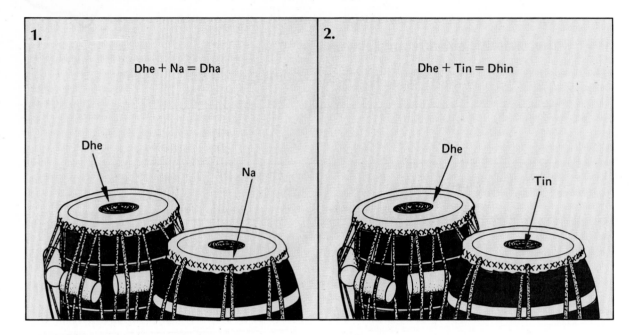

1.

Dhe + Na = Dha

Dhe

Na

2.

Dhe + Tin = Dhin

Dhe

Tin

INDIAN DRUM SYLLABLES

Dhe (pronounced *dhuh*)—left-hand (low) drum struck just above the middle

Na (pronounced *nah*)—right-hand (high) drum struck near the edge

Tin—right-hand drum struck near the middle

Dha (pronounced *dhah*)—*Dhe* and *Na* performed at the same time

Dhin—*Dhe* and *Tin* performed at the same time

Chant the syllables while playing this pattern on low and high drums.

Dha Dhin Dhin Dha Dha Dhin Dhin Dha Dha Tin Tin Na Na Dhin Dhin Dha

Alla Rakha

138

Joy to the World

WORDS AND MUSIC BY HOYT AXTON

1. Jer - e - mi - ah was a bull - frog, Was a good __ friend of

mine. Nev - er un - der - stood a sin - gle word he said, __ but we

al - ways had a might - y fine time. __

Yes, we al - ways had a might - y fine time.

Sing - ing joy to the world. All __ the boys and girls __ now.

Joy to the fish - es in the deep blue sea. __ Joy to __ you and me. __

2. If I were the king of the world, tell you what I'd do,
Throw away the fears and the tears and the jeers,
And have a good time with you.
Yes, I'd have a good time with you. *Refrain.*

Countermelody for B

Sing - ing joy to the world, Joy to the world;

Joy, joy, joy, joy, Joy to __ you and me. __

Naughty Little Flea

WORDS AND MUSIC BY NORMAN THOMAS

TRANSCRIBED FROM THE RECORDING BY MIRIAM MAKEBA AND HARRY BELAFONTE   © 1957 PINEBROOK MUSIC CORP. C/O H/B WEBMAN & COMPANY. USED BY PERMISSION.

(A) REFRAIN

Where did the naught-y lit - tle flea go?

Won't some-bod-y tell me? Where did the naught-y lit - tle

flea go? Won't some - bod - y tell me?

(B)

1. There was a naught-y lit - tle flea; He climbed up on the

dog - gie's knee; He climbed some here, he climbed some there;

He was climb - ing ev - 'ry - where. Tell me,

2. He climbed some here,
   he climbed some there;
   He was climbing everywhere.
   And now at last he's found a nest
   Where he can get some food and rest. Tell me, . . .

3. He bit him here, he bit him there;
   He bit him almost everywhere.
   When he was done he wanted more;
   He never tasted such a dog before.
   Tell me, . . .

Listen for this rhythm pattern when the vowels are chanted

in *A-E-I-O-U.* Clap each time the vowel sounds are chanted.

A-E-I-O-U

Listen to these pieces. Do you hear mostly short sounds, mostly long sounds, or short and long sounds together? Each time a number is called, decide which of the three answers is correct. Choose the answer that best describes what is happening in the music.

---

1   MOSTLY   MOSTLY   SHORT AND
         SHORT   LONG   LONG TOGETHER

Stockhausen: *Klavierstück*

---

2   MOSTLY   MOSTLY   SHORT AND
         SHORT   LONG   LONG TOGETHER

Mendelssohn: *Nocturne*

---

3   MOSTLY   MOSTLY   SHORT AND
         SHORT   LONG   LONG TOGETHER

Tchaikovsky: *Capriccio Italien*

---

4   MOSTLY   MOSTLY   SHORT AND
         SHORT   LONG   LONG TOGETHER

Vivaldi: *The Four Seasons,* "Winter"

---

5   MOSTLY   MOSTLY   SHORT AND
         SHORT   LONG   LONG TOGETHER

Goin' down the Road Feeling Bad

THREE SOUNDS TO A BEAT

Notice the triplet ♪♪♪ in each phrase as you sing this song
about a very strange mosquito.

The Mosquito

FOLK SONG FROM COLOMBIA   ENGLISH WORDS BY MARGARET MARKS

1. I went to the Sie-rra Blan-ca   To hunt with my dog, Pe-rri-to,

When sud-den-ly I en-count-ered   a great o-ver-grown mos-qui-to.

I dropped to my knees and fired,___   And star-tled by that ex-plo-sion,

The an-i-mal lost his bal-ance   And tum-bled in-to the o-cean.

2. So huge was this big mosquito,
A tidal wave swelled the water,
His head lay in Cádiz harbor,
His feet lay across Gibraltar.
And then the ordeal was over,
The bug ceased to make a motion,
I called for a crane and derrick,
You've never seen such commotion.

3. They made from his hide ten thousand
High boots of the finest leather,
And just from the bits left over,
A hundred or so umbrellas;
And even now, ten years later,
Though nothing could seem absurder,
The whole of the Spanish Army
Is eating mosquito-burger!

Can you hear triplets in this piece for piano?

Mozart: *Variations on "Ah, vous dirai-je, Maman?"*

142

PIECE FOR RECORDER OR BELLS

Look at the score to find places where you will play triplets—
three sounds to one beat.

Din, Don   FOLK MELODY FROM SPAIN

MUSICAL SETTING FROM THE BABY'S SONG BOOK © 1971 ELIZABETH POSTON. USED BY PERMISSION OF THOMAS Y. CROWELL AND THE BODLEY HEAD.

RECORDERS OR BELLS

While you play the melody on recorder or bells, have others
play the percussion parts.

Wood Block

Finger Cymbals

WORD RHYTHMS

The kookaburra is a bird found in Australia. Its name, like
yours, has a special rhythm pattern. Tap the rhythm of
"kookaburra." Now tap the patterns made by the words of the
whole song.

Kookaburra

WORDS AND MUSIC BY MARION SINCLAIR

FROM THE DITTY BAG, COMPILED BY JANET E. TOBITT. USED WITH PERMISSION.

Kook - a - bur - ra sits on the old gum tree,_____

Mer - ry, mer - ry king of the bush is he, _____

Laugh, kook - a - bur - ra, laugh, kook - a - bur - ra, Gay your life must be.

Choose one of these rhythm patterns to play on a percussion
instrument throughout "Kookaburra."

SOUND PIECE 7: Intersections

DAVID S. WALKER

Each vertical column in the score stands for one beat.

Follow the red, green, or purple line to see where the beat is divided. Is the beat divided into two, three, or four sounds?

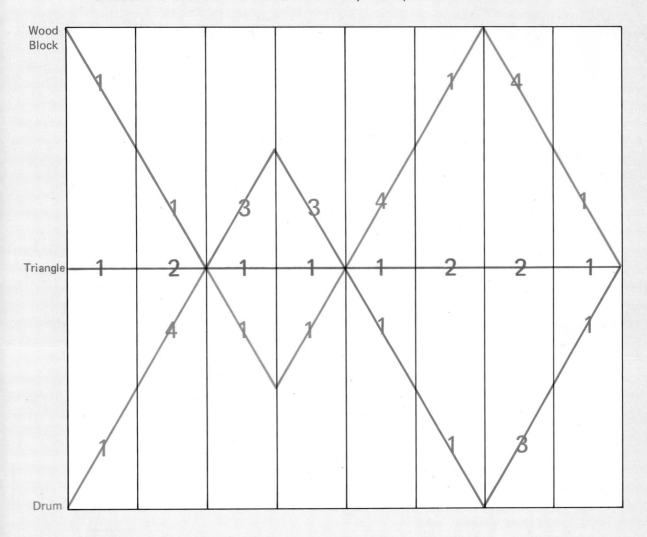

Choose one of the parts to play. Team up with two others to perform your version of *Sound Piece 7*.

A PATTERN THAT REPEATS

Look at the rhythm pattern made by the notes in the color box.

How many times do you find the pattern in this song?

Ta-ra-ra Boom-de-ay

WORDS AND MUSIC BY HENRY SAYERS

Ta - ra - ra boom - de - ay, Ta - ra - ra boom - de - ay,

Ta - ra - ra boom - de - ay, Ta - ra - ra boom - de - ay,

Ta - ra - ra boom - de - ay, Ta - ra - ra boom - de - ay,

Ta - ra - ra boom - de - ay, Ta - ra - ra boom - de - ay._____

A NEW NOTE

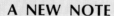

F#

Practice this new note on the recorder. Then play this part as others sing "Ta-ra-ra Boom-de-ay."

Be sure to play dotted rhythms.

Recorder or Bells

F#   G

146

Red, Red Robin

WORDS AND MUSIC BY HARRY WOODS

When the red, red rob-in comes bob, bob, bob-bin' a-long, a-

long, There'll be no more sob-bin' when he starts throb-bin' his old sweet

song. "Wake up, wake up, you sleep-y head! Get up, get up, get out_ of bed;

Cheer up, cheer up, the sun_ is red; Live, love, laugh and be hap-py!"

What if I've been blue, now I'm walk-in' through fields of flowers;

Rain may glis-ten but still I'll lis-ten for hours and hours.

I'm just a kid a-gain, do-in' what I did a-gain, Sing - ing a

song, When the red, red rob-in comes bob, bob, bob-bin' a-long.____

SYNCOPATION—A SPECIAL SOUND

Listen to the recording and notice the rhythm pattern made by
the notes in the color boxes.

Let the Sun Shine Down on Me

WORDS AND MUSIC BY 'THAN HALL

FROM JEAN RITCHIE: CELEBRATION OF LIFE—HER SONGS, HER POEMS. © 1963 & 1971. PUBLISHED BY GEORDIE MUSIC PUBLISHING, INC. USED BY PERMISSION.

O, roll on, clouds in the morn - in', Roll on, clouds in the

morn - in'; Roll on, clouds in the morn - in', Let the

sun shine down on me.
1. I looked out this morn - in',
2. I know there's a great day com - in', When

Deep - down trou - ble I see; Yes, I looked out this
no more trou - ble I see; When we'll all shout to -

morn - in', Let the sun shine down on me.
geth - er, Let the sun shine down on me.

Tap these rhythm patterns. Can you hear and feel the difference
between syncopation and no syncopation?

1. sun shine down on me.
2. sun shine down on me.

148

A SYNCOPATED PATTERN

Tinga Layo

CALYPSO FROM THE WEST INDIES   ENGLISH VERSION BY MARGARET MARKS

(A) REFRAIN

Tin - ga Lay - o!   Run, lit - tle don - key, run!

¡Ven, mi bu - rri - to, ven!

1.-3.   *Last time only*

Tin - ga Lay - o!   Run, lit - tle don - key, run! run!

¡Ven, mi bu - rri - to, ven! ven!

(B) VERSE

1. My don - key yes, my don - key no,
1. *Bu - rri - to sí, bu - rri - to no.*

My don - key stop when I tell him to go!

¡Bu - rri - to co - me con te - ne - dor!

2. My donkey hee, my donkey haw,
   My donkey sit on the kitchen floor! *Refrain*

3. My donkey kick, my donkey balk,
   My donkey eat with a silver fork! *Refrain*

Play one of these patterns throughout the song.

Which one uses syncopation?

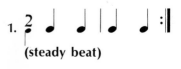

1. (steady beat)

2. Tin-ga Lay - o! Tin-ga

3. Run, lit - tle don-key, run!

149

A LIVELY SONG

Syncopated patterns add to the spirit of this lively song.

Feel the syncopation every time you sing the phrase *See, can't you jump for joy.*

See, Can't You Jump for Joy   BLACK-AMERICAN RING SHOUT

My Lord calls me, See, can't you jump   for joy, ————

See, can't you jump   for joy, ——

See, can't you jump   for joy. ——

My Lord calls me, See, can't you jump   for joy, ——

Broth-er, can't you jump for joy. ——

Do a stamp-clap pattern as you sing the song.

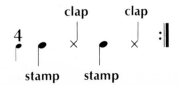

150

A QUIET SONG

Syncopation is sometimes used in quiet songs. Listen to this
song. In which section can you feel syncopation, A or B?

Grandpa

WORDS AND MUSIC BY CHRIS DEDRICK   © 1972 ALMITRA MUSIC COMPANY, INC.

(A) VERSE

1. Grand - pa   is   a   qui - et   name   for   a   ver - y   qui - et   man.
2. Get   to   know your grand - pa,   you   can__ learn   a   lot   from   him.

And   no   one   else   re - mem-bers   all   the   things that Grand - pa   can.
His   know - ledge   has   a   beau - ty   like   the   leaves   up - on   a   limb.

Sto - ries   full   of   truth - ful - ness   that   time   can - not   e - rase
Like   the   leaf,   a   pat - tern,___   and   like   the   branch,   a   strength,

Are   writ - ten   out   like   gos - pel   in   the   wrin - kles   of   his   face.
For,   like   the   tree,   he's breathed the   wind   and watched the world   at   length.

[B] REFRAIN *(Repeat refrain last time.)*

Grand - pa, Grand - pa - pa, ___   Grand - pa - pa - pa, ___

Grand - pa - pa - pa - pa. _____

3.   Sometimes you can sit with him and never say a word.

You start to think of silence as a sound that can be heard,

And, hearing it, you're led into a diff'rent place to live

Where nothing scares or hurts you, and there's nothing to forgive.

Listen to these pieces.

Do you hear syncopation, or no syncopation?

Each time a number is called, decide which of the two
answers is correct. Choose the answer that best describes
what is happening in the music.

1 SYNCOPATION   NO SYNCOPATION   Joplin: *The Entertainer*

2 SYNCOPATION   NO SYNCOPATION   Hays: *Arabella Rag*

3 SYNCOPATION   NO SYNCOPATION   Handel: *Sonata in F*

4 SYNCOPATION   NO SYNCOPATION   Debussy: *Golliwog's Cake Walk*

5 SYNCOPATION   NO SYNCOPATION   *Find the Ring*

6 SYNCOPATION   NO SYNCOPATION   Malinke Tribe: *Drum Duet*

FOUR PHRASES, ONE PATTERN

What can you discover in the phrases of this song about our
beautiful country? The first phrase is shown in the color box.

America, the Beautiful

MUSIC BY SAMUEL A. WARD   WORDS BY KATHARINE LEE BATES

O beau - ti - ful for spa - cious skies, For am - ber waves of grain,
O beau - ti - ful for pa - triot dream That sees be - yond the years

For pur - ple moun - tain maj - es - ties A - bove the fruit - ed plain!
Thine al - a - bas - ter cit - ies gleam, Un-dimmed by hu - man tears!

A - mer - i - ca! A - mer - i - ca! God shed His grace on thee

And crown thy good with broth - er - hood From sea to shin - ing sea!

Recorder or Bells Countermelody

PLAY A PATTERN

Will you accompany "Clementine" with a dotted-rhythm

pattern, or with the triplet pattern?

Clementine

AMERICAN FOLK SONG

1. In a cav - ern, in a can - yon, Ex - ca - vat - ing for a mine,
2. Light she was, and like a fair - y, And her shoes were num - ber nine,
3. Drove she duck - lings to the wa - ter Ev - 'ry morn - ing just at nine,

Dwelt a min - er, for - ty - nin - er, And his daugh - ter, Clem - en - tine.
Her - ring box - es with - out top - ses, San - dals were for Clem - en - tine.
Hit her foot a - gainst a splin - ter, Fell in - to the foam - ing brine.

REFRAIN

(optional harmony part)

Oh, my dar - ling, oh, my dar - ling, Oh, my dar - ling Clem - en - tine,

You are lost and gone for - ev - er, Dread - ful sor - ry, Clem - en - tine.

Sticks (Play four times.)

Tambourine (Play four times.) (shake)

Autoharp

154

WHAT DO YOU HEAR?   14: Rhythm Patterns

Listen to these pieces. Each time a number is called, decide
which pattern you are hearing.

1 — *The Mosquito*

2 — Mozart: *Symphony No. 40*

3 — *America, the Beautiful*

4 — Haydn: *String Quartet*, Op. 76

5 — Tchaikovsky: *Symphony No. 6*

6 — Beethoven: *Symphony No. 7*

REPEATED SHAPES AND LINES

What do these drawings show? For a clue, look at pages 156 and 157.

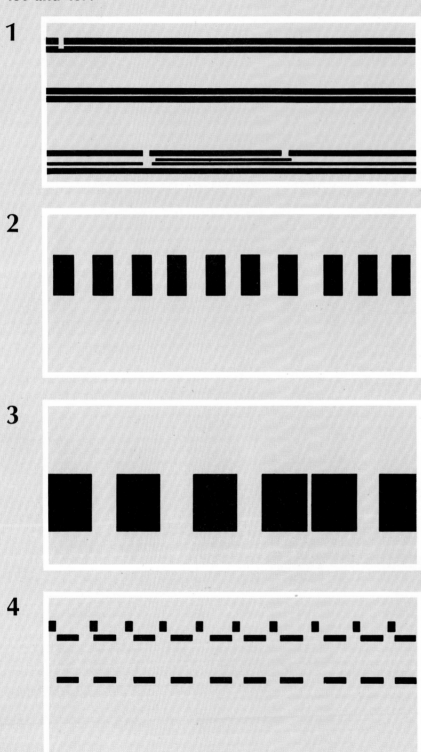

REPEATED RHYTHM PATTERN

This rhythm pattern is from a song that you know.

Can you name the song?

What do these lines show? Clue: Look at the song on page 142.

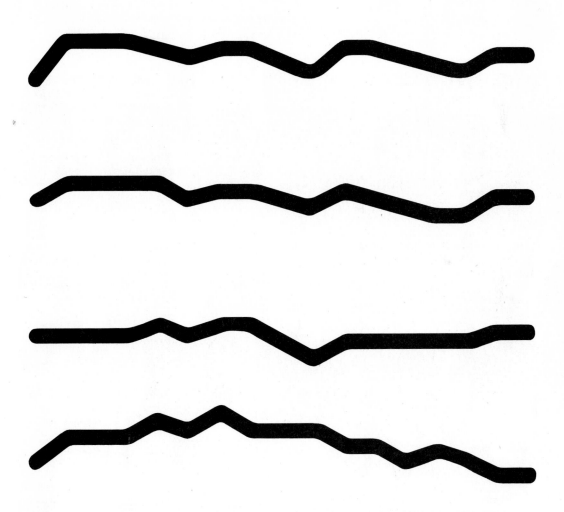

A painting can have pattern, line, and direction. Can a piece of music have pattern, line, and direction also?

◎ Chopin: *Prelude in A Minor*
7

Tone Color

VOICES

In the recording of *Swing Low, Sweet Chariot,* you hear both women's and men's voices. Who sings the solo parts, a man or a woman?

🎵 *Swing Low, Sweet Chariot*
7

All Hid

Add the tone color of *your* voice to the voices on the recording.

YOUR VOICE

Your voice has a tone color all its own. Whether you speak, sing, shout, or whisper, no one else's voice sounds exactly like yours. Use your natural speaking voice when you say this poem.

> Windy winter rain . . .
> My silly big umbrella
> Tries walking backward.
>
> Shisei-Jo

Now try using your voice in unusual ways.

Look at the notation for the sound piece on p. 163. Notice that the score uses symbols to stand for different voice sounds. The legend below tells what the symbols mean.

LEGEND

Ȼ   Blow.

ϕ   Whistle.

⸭   Whisper.

∞   Make the sound continue.

⫪   Make unvoiced lip and mouth sounds without breathing out.

SOUND PIECE 8: Windy Winter Rain ALLEN BRINGS

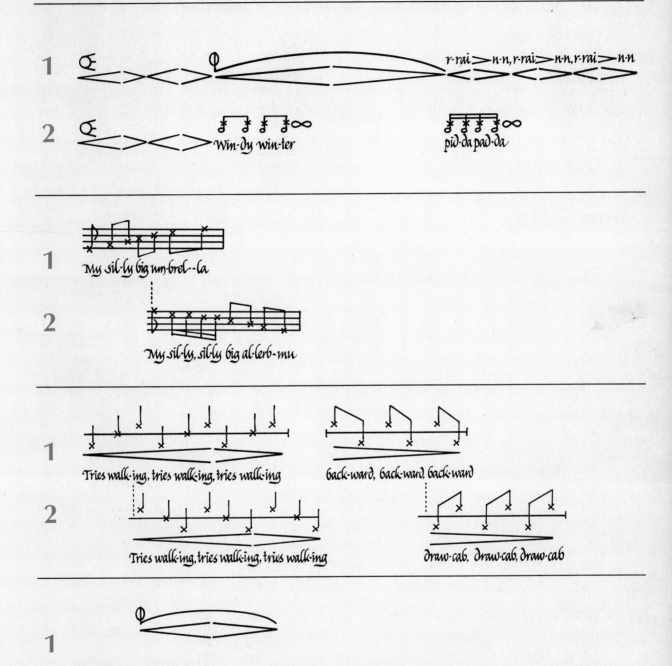

SINGING A STORY

Use your *speaking voice* and read the story of Don Gato, the lovesick cat.

Now use your *singing voice* to tell the story. (In music, a song that tells a story is called a *ballad.*) Decide how you will use dynamics and tempo to dramatize what happened to Señor Don Gato.

Don Gato

FOLK SONG FROM MEXICO   ENGLISH WORDS BY MARGARET MARKS

1. Oh, Se - ñor Don Ga - to was a cat,_____
2. "I a - dore you!" wrote the la - dy cat,_____

On a high, red roof Don Ga - to sat._____
Who was fluff - y, white, and nice and fat._____

He went there to read a let - ter, meow, meow, meow,
There was not a sweet - er kit - ty, meow, meow, meow,

Where the read - ing light was bet - ter,
In the coun - try or the cit - y,

'Twas a love note for Don Ga - to!_____
And she said she'd wed Don Ga - to!_____

164

3. Oh, Don Gato jumped so happily
   He fell off the roof and broke his knee,
   Broke his ribs and all his whiskers, . . .
   And his little solar plexus, . . .
   "¡Ay carramba!" cried Don Gato!

4. Then the doctors all came on the run
   Just to see if something could be done,
   And they held a consultation, . . .
   About how to save their patient, . . .
   How to save Señor Don Gato!

5. But in spite of everything they tried
   Poor Señor Don Gato up and died,
   Oh, it wasn't very merry, . . .
   Going to the cemetery, . . .
   For the ending of Don Gato!

6. When the funeral passed the market square
   Such a smell of fish was in the air,
   Though his burial was slated, . . .
   He became re-animated! . . .
   He came back to life, Don Gato!

SOUND EFFECTS

Make up a sound effect for each of these symbols. You can use
your voice, a percussion instrument, or both.

When you are ready, add the sound effects when you sing
about Don Gato.

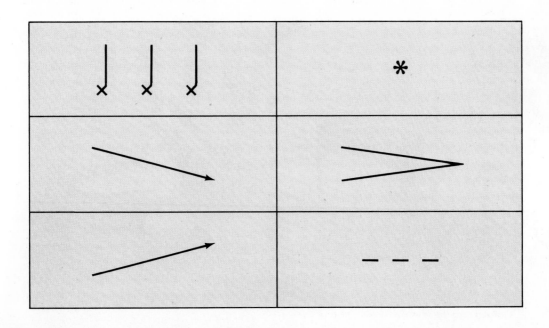

PERCUSSION INSTRUMENTS

Listen to an ensemble of percussion instruments in this recording.

🎯 McKenzie: *Samba*

You have played percussion instruments to accompany many songs that you know. Decide on a song, then choose a percussion instrument to play while the class sings along.

AN OLD MOUNTAIN SONG

Choose a percussion instrument to play during the long sounds in this old mountain song.

She'll Be Comin' Round the Mountain

SOUTHERN MOUNTAIN SONG

1. She'll be com - in' round the moun - tain when she comes,_____
2. She'll be driv - in' six white hor - ses when she comes,_____

She'll be com - in' round the moun - tain when she comes,_____
She'll be driv - in' six white hor - ses when she comes,_____

She'll be com - in' round the moun - tain,
She'll be driv - in' six white hor - ses,

She'll be com - in' round the moun - tain,
She'll be driv - in' six white hor - ses,

She'll be com - in' round the moun - tain when she comes._____
She'll be driv - in' six white hor - ses when she comes._____

3. Oh, we'll kill the old red rooster when she comes, . . .

4. Oh, we'll all have chicken and dumplings when she comes, . . .

5. Oh, we'll all go out to meet her when she comes, . . .

Follow the chord names in the music to play an accompaniment on the Autoharp. You will use the chords G, D₇, C.

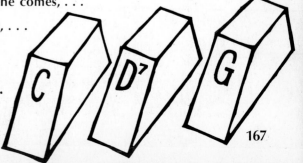

167

PARTS FOR PERCUSSION

Play these percussion parts to accompany "Hotsia!"

In each part, silently say the numbers in time with the steady beat.

Play the instrument whenever you say a large-size number.

Cowbell

1 2 3 4 5 6 7 8 9 10 11 12

High Drum

1 2 3 4 5 6 7 8 9 10 11 12

Rattle

1 2 3 4 5 6 7 8 9 10 11 12

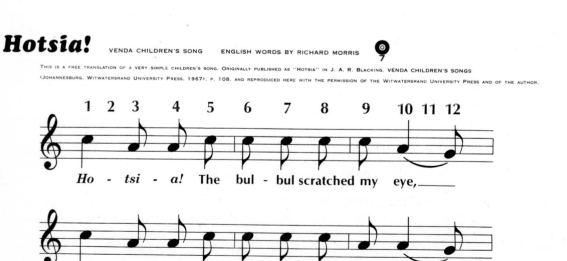

Hotsia!

VENDA CHILDREN'S SONG   ENGLISH WORDS BY RICHARD MORRIS

THIS IS A FREE TRANSLATION OF A VERY SIMPLE CHILDREN'S SONG. ORIGINALLY PUBLISHED AS "HOTSIA" IN J. A. R. BLACKING. VENDA CHILDREN'S SONGS (JOHANNESBURG, WITWATERSRAND UNIVERSITY PRESS, 1967), P. 108, AND REPRODUCED HERE WITH THE PERMISSION OF THE WITWATERSRAND UNIVERSITY PRESS AND OF THE AUTHOR.

1 2 3 4 5 6 7 8 9 10 11 12

Ho - tsi - a! The bul - bul scratched my eye,____

Ho - tsi - a! It hurts so, I could cry.____

168

Ho - tsi - a! How can you laugh that way?____

Ho - tsi - a! You're not my friend to - day.____

Ho - tsi - a! Oh, did - n't we have fun?____

Ho - tsi - a! How those ba - boons did run____

Ho - tsi - a! From old Ne - khum - be's gar - den,

Ho - tsi - a! When we all yelled and chased them

Ho - tsi - a! Back up in - to the moun - tains.

The word *hotsia* means "sneeze." In Africa this sound is supposed to frighten away birds, baboons, and other pests that eat the crops. When you sing the song, use your voice to imitate a sneeze.

If you haven't tried it yet, practice the "African Rhythm Complex" on pages 88 and 89. It also moves in a 12-beat phrase.

AUTOHARP ACCOMPANIMENTS

Play an Autoharp accompaniment for one or two of these old favorites. The recording will give you ideas for playing different strums.

SKIP TO MY LOU   AMERICAN GAME SONG

1. <u>Flies</u> in the buttermilk, shoo, fly, shoo!
   Flies in the buttermilk, shoo, fly, shoo!
   Flies in the buttermilk, shoo, fly, shoo!
   Skip to my Lou, my darling.

2. Little red wagon painted blue,

3. Lost my partner, what'll I do?

4. I'll get another, better than you!

BILLY BOY   FOLK SONG FROM ENGLAND

1. Oh, <u>where</u> have you been, Billy Boy, Billy Boy?
   Oh, where have you been, charming Billy?
   I have been to seek a wife,
   She's the joy of my life,
   She's a young thing and cannot leave her mother.

2. Did she bid you to come in, Billy Boy, Billy Boy?
   Did she bid you to come in, charming Billy?
   Yes, she bid me to come in,
   There's a dimple in her chin,
   She's a young thing and cannot leave her mother.

3. Did she give you a chair, Billy Boy, Billy Boy?
   Yes, she gave me a chair,
   But there was no bottom there . . .

4. Can she make a cherry pie, Billy Boy, Billy Boy?
   She can make a cherry pie,
   Quick as a cat can wink her eye . . .

5. Can she cook and can she spin, Billy Boy, Billy Boy?
   She can cook and she can spin,
   She can do most anything . . .

6. How old is she, Billy Boy, Billy Boy?
   Three times six and four times seven,
   Twenty-eight and eleven . . .

POLLY WOLLY DOODLE

AMERICAN FOLK SONG

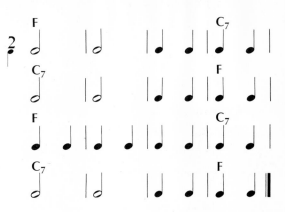

1. Oh, I <u>went</u> down South for to see my Sal,
   Singing Polly Wolly Doodle all the day;
   My Sal, she is a spunky gal,
   Singing Polly Wolly Doodle all the day.

Refrain
   Fare thee well, fare thee well,
   Fare thee well my fairy fay,
   For I'm goin' to Louisiana, for to see my Susyanna,
   Singing Polly Wolly Doodle all the day.

2. Oh, my Sal, she is a maiden fair,
   Singing Polly Wolly Doodle all the day;
   With curly eyes and laughing hair,
   Singing Polly Wolly Doodle all the day.

3. The partridge is a pretty bird,
   It has a speckled breast,
   It steals away the farmer's grain,
   And totes it to its nest!

4. The raccoon's tail is ringed around,
   The 'possum's tail is bare,
   The rabbit's got no tail at all,
   Just a little bitty bunch of hair!

5. The June-bug he has golden wings,
   The lightning bug totes a flame,
   The caterpillar's got no wings at all,
   But he gets there just the same!

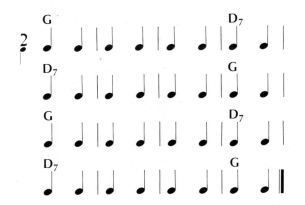

AIN'T GONNA RAIN

AMERICAN FOLK SONG

1. The <u>wood</u>chuck, he's a-choppin' wood,
   The 'possum, he's a-haulin'.
   My poor old dog fell off a log
   And killed himself a-bawlin'.

Refrain
   It ain't gonna rain, it ain't gonna rain,
   It ain't gonna rain no more.
   Come on down, ev'rybody sing.
   It ain't gonna rain no more.

2. Just bake them biscuits good and brown,
   It ain't gonna rain no more.
   Swing your ladies round and round,
   It ain't gonna rain no more.

3. I'll tune the fiddle, you get the bow,
   It ain't gonna rain no more.
   The weatherman just told me so,
   It ain't gonna rain no more.

4. Oh, what did the blackbird say to the crow?
   "It ain't gonna rain no more.
   It ain't gonna hail, it ain't gonna snow,
   It ain't gonna rain no more."

RECORDERS

Soprano

Alto

Tenor

Bass

Listen to a soprano recorder as it plays in a consort, or group. The soprano recorder plays in a higher register than the alto, tenor, and bass recorders.

 In Dulci Jubilo
8

The soprano recorder part you heard is notated below. Practice the part so you can play along with the recording. You will need a new tone, high E.

A NEW NOTE

E

In Dulci Jubilo   GERMAN MELODY

BRASS INSTRUMENTS

You have heard the tone color of recorders playing in an ensemble. The tone colors of brass instruments can be combined in an ensemble also. Listen to this music for brass ensemble.

8 M. Franck: *Intrada II*

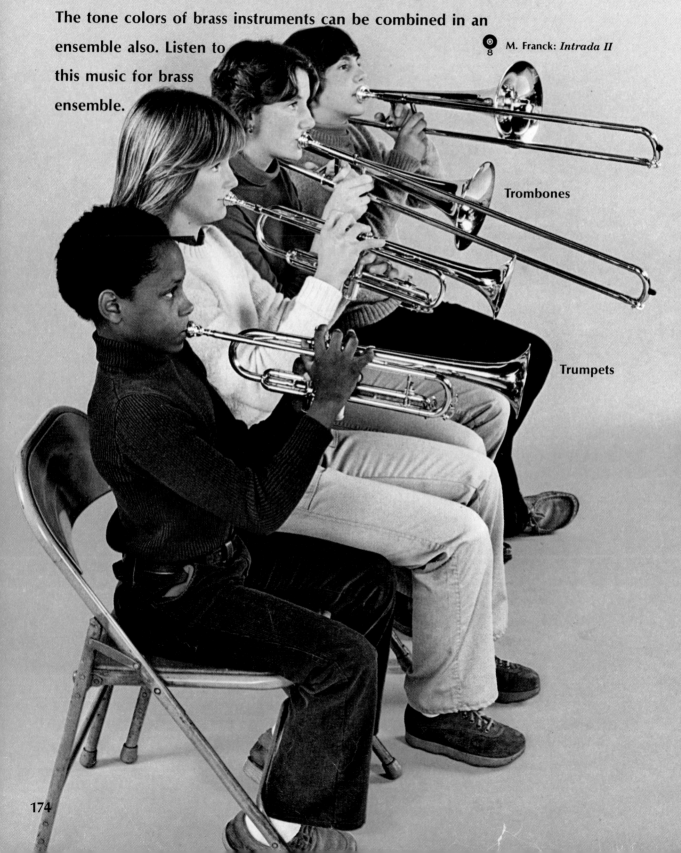

Trombones

Trumpets

America

TRADITIONAL MELODY   WORDS BY SAMUEL FRANCIS SMITH

Sing along with the brass ensemble on the recording of this

well-known patriotic song.

My coun - try! 'tis of thee, Sweet land of lib - er - ty,
Our fa - thers' God, to Thee, Au - thor of lib - er - ty,

Of thee I sing; Land where my fa - thers died,
To Thee we sing; Long may our land be bright

Land of the Pil - grim's pride, From ev - 'ry___ moun - tain - side
With free - dom's ho - ly light; Pro - tect___ us___ by Thy might,

Let___ free - dom ring!
Great___ God, our King!

If you play trumpet, practice the part below. Then play along

with the brass ensemble on the recording of version 2 of "America."

Trumpet

WOODWIND QUINTET

Listen to the tone color of a
woodwind quintet. The picture shows
the instruments that make up the
ensemble.

How many instruments play in a
quintet? Which instrument plays the
highest sounds? Which instrument
plays the lowest sounds?

Ibert: *Trois pièces brèves*, No. 3
8

If you play the clarinet or flute,
practice the parts for "America" to
play for the class. You might want to
invite the class to sing along.

Flute

AMERICA   TRADITIONAL

Clarinet

Oboe

French Horn

Clarinet

Bassoon

Countermelody

Flute

STRING INSTRUMENTS

Mozart: *String Quartet in D Minor*

Violins

Viola

Cello

What instrument would you expect to hear with this fiddle tune?

The Frog in the Well

FOLK SONG FROM THE SOUTHERN APPALACHIANS

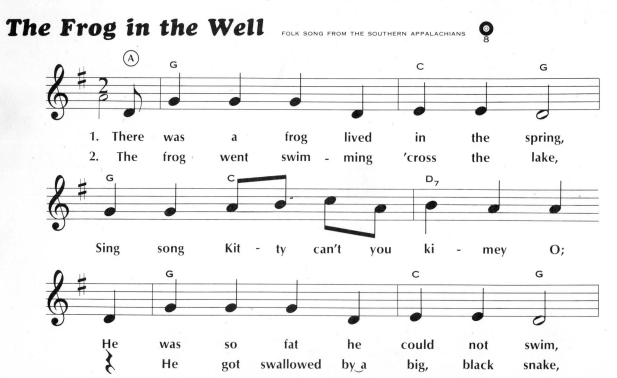

1. There was a frog lived in the spring,
2. The frog went swim - ming 'cross the lake,

Sing song Kit - ty can't you ki - mey O;

He was so fat he could not swim,
He got swallowed by a big, black snake,

178

Sing song Kit - ty can't you ki - mey O.

Kee - mey O ma ki - mey O ma dir - ey O ma wear,

Me hi, me ho, me in come Sal - ly Sin - gle,

Some time Pen-ny Win-kle, In stepped nip cat, Hit him with a brick bat,

Sing song Kit - ty can't you ki - mey O.

If you play violin, add its tone color to section A of "The Frog in the Well." Choose one of the parts below to play. Will you bow the strings, or pluck them?

Section A

1.

Section A

2.

KEYBOARD INSTRUMENTS

Listen to two keyboard instruments
playing the same piece.
Neither instrument is the piano.
Are the tone colors of the two
instruments the same, or different?

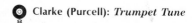 Clarke (Purcell): *Trumpet Tune*

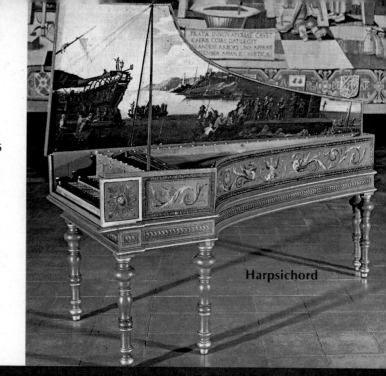

Harpsichord

Piano

Pipe Organ

ELECTRONIC
INSTRUMENTS

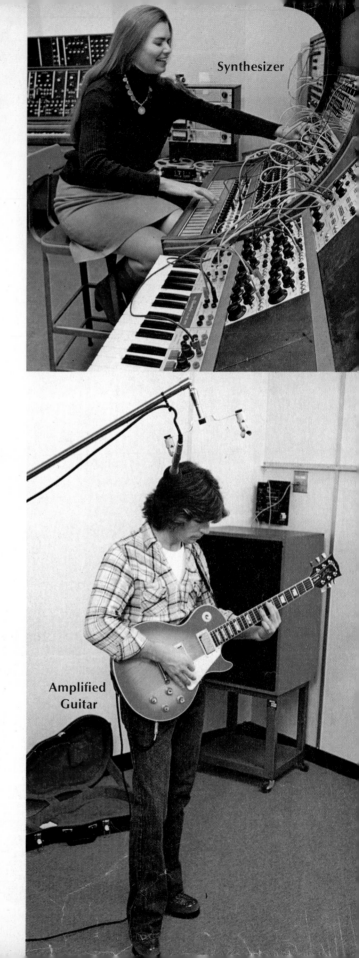

Synthesizer

Composers have always been fascinated by new possibilities for sounds. They are always looking for new ways to produce sounds and new ways to put sounds together.

On this recording you will hear "Old Blue" performed on two different instruments—a synthesizer and an amplified guitar. Which instrument plays first?

◉ *Electronic Old Blue*
8

Amplified
Guitar

WHAT DO YOU HEAR?   15: Tone Color 🎱

Can you hear tone
color in music?
Listen to these pieces.
Each time a number is
called, decide which
answer is correct.
Listen. Then choose
your answer.

1
PERCUSSION
VOICES
KEYBOARD
RECORDERS
BRASS
STRINGS
WOODWINDS

Five Villancicos, No. 4

2
PERCUSSION
VOICES
KEYBOARD
RECORDERS
BRASS
STRINGS
WOODWINDS

For the Beauty of the Earth

3
PERCUSSION
VOICES
KEYBOARD
RECORDERS
BRASS
STRINGS
WOODWINDS

Webern: *Five Movements
for String Quartet*, Op. 5, No. 3

4
PERCUSSION
VOICES
KEYBOARD
RECORDERS
BRASS
STRINGS
WOODWINDS

Joplin: *The Entertainer*

5
PERCUSSION
VOICES
KEYBOARD
RECORDERS
BRASS
STRINGS
WOODWINDS

McKenzie: *Three Dances*, "Samba"

6
PERCUSSION
VOICES
KEYBOARD
RECORDERS
BRASS
STRINGS
WOODWINDS

Bach: *Fugue in G Minor*

7
PERCUSSION
VOICES
KEYBOARD
RECORDERS
BRASS
STRINGS
WOODWINDS

Locke: *Courante*

8
PERCUSSION
VOICES
KEYBOARD
RECORDERS
BRASS
STRINGS
WOODWINDS

Pierne: *Pastorale*

PLAYING PERCUSSION INSTRUMENTS

Boys and girls in Puerto Rico play percussion instruments to
accompany Christmas carols. Use maracas, bongos, and claves, and
create your own percussion parts. Then play along with the recording.

Hurry, Good Shepherds

Pastores a Belén CHRISTMAS SONG FROM PUERTO RICO

ENGLISH VERSION BY VERNE MUÑOZ

Oh, hur - ry on your way;____ Good shep - herds, hur - ry to see Him.
Pas - to - res, a Be - lén____ Va - mos con a - le - grí - a;

The Son of Mar - y waits;____ Good shep - herds, hur - ry to greet Him.
Que ha na - ci - do ya____ El Hi - jo de____ Ma - rí - a.

In Beth - le - hem,____ the bless - ed Ba - by lies.____
A - llí,____ a - llí,____ Nos es - pe - ra Je - sús.

In Beth - le - hem,____ the bless - ed Ba - by lies.____
A - llí,____ a - llí,____ Nos es - pe - ra Je - sús.

Bring hon - ey sweet for Mar - y's Son, And al - mond cakes for ev - 'ry - one.
Lle - ve - mos pues tu - rro - nes y miel Pa - ra o - fre - cer al Ni - ño Man - uel,

Bring hon - ey sweet for Mar - y's Son, And al - mond cakes for ev - 'ry - one.
Lle - ve - mos pues tu - rro - nes y miel Pa - ra o - fre - cer al Ni - ño Man - uel.

Hur - ry, hur - ry, do not de - lay, Greet___ the Ba - by born___ this day,___
Va - mos, va - mos, va - mos a ver, Va - mos a ver al re - cién na - ci - do,

Greet___ the Ba - by born___ this day.
Va - mos a ver al Ni - ño Man - uel.

Purim Song

HASIDIC FOLK MELODY   ENGLISH WORDS BY ELIZABETH S. BACHMAN

Come a - long, come a - long, Sing a mer - ry Pu - rim song.

Cel - e - brate, cel - e - brate, Joy - ous hol - i - day.

Come, twirl the gra - ger round and round; Let's fill the room with hap - py sound;

Now pass the ha - man - tash - en round; Joy - ous hol - i - day.

Play these percussion parts to accompany "Purim Song."

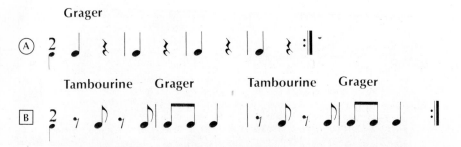

Grager

Tambourine   Grager   Tambourine   Grager

Style: Jazz

Here are some musical qualities that are used in the style called *jazz*.

LOUD   SOFT

FAST   SLOW

BIG BAND   SMALL COMBO

            IMPROVISATION

Listen to these jazz pieces. For each one, decide which qualities you hear.

8 Lewis and Gillespie: *Two Bass Hit*

8 Kern: *Yesterdays*

8 Selden: *The Magic Bus Ate My Doughnut*

186

CALL CHART 8: Jazz 🎵 8

Listen to the recording. As each number is called, look at the chart.
It will help you to hear what is going on in the music.

Olson and Staton: *All I Recall Is You*

---

1 SOFT, MODERATE TEMPO, PIANO IMPROVISES

---

2 BIG BAND ENTERS, GETS LOUDER

---

3 BASS INSTRUMENT IMPROVISES—BAND ACCOMPANIES

---

4 SAXOPHONE IMPROVISES, GETS SOFTER

---

5 DRUM IMPROVISES

---

6 BIG BAND ENTERS, GETS LOUDER

---

7 GETS SOFTER, THEN LOUDER

---

8 ENDS SOFT

Melody

188

STEPS, LEAPS, REPEATS

Play these bell patterns to accompany "Evening." Which one has tones that leap? Tones that repeat? Tones that move by step?

1. D E F G A

2. low D high D

3. A

Evening

FOLK MELODY FROM HUNGARY   ENGLISH WORDS BY ROSEMARY JACQUES

p

Voic - es fill the eve - ning air   with their hap - py sing - ing,

Joy and laugh-ter ev - 'ry-where through the land are ring - ing.

p   *p*

Cast - ing all their cares a - way,   Danc - ers whirl till

f

break of day.   Hear the mu - sic play.

p

Voic - es fill the eve - ning air   with their hap - py sing - ing,

p

Joy and laugh-ter ev - 'ry-where through the land are ring - ing.

189

CONTOUR—THE SHAPE OF A MELODY

A melody can have tones that move upward or downward by step, tones that leap, and tones that repeat. The way the tones move gives the melody a shape, or contour.

How do the tones move in each of the color boxes? Find other places in section B where tones move in the same way.

Rookoombine

FOLK SONG FROM JAMAICA

MELODY AND WORDS OF FIRST VERSE FROM FOLK SONGS OF JAMAICA, EDITED AND ARRANGED BY TOM MURRAY. COPYRIGHT 1952 BY THE OXFORD UNIVERSITY PRESS, LONDON; WORDS OF SECOND VERSE FROM FOLK SONGS OF THE CARIBBEAN BY JIM MORSE. COPYRIGHT © 1958 BY BANTAM BOOKS. USED BY PERMISSION.

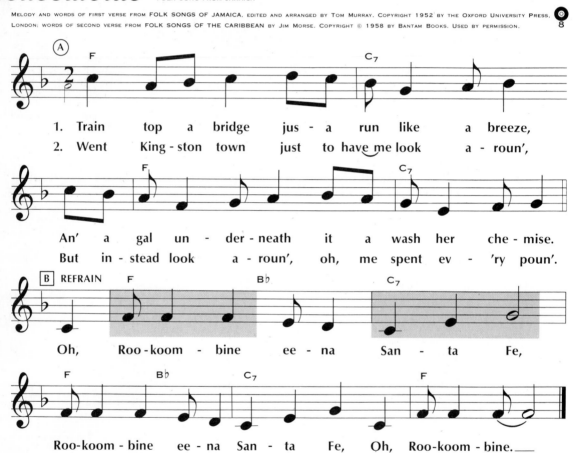

1. Train top a bridge jus - a run like a breeze,
2. Went King - ston town just to have me look a - roun',

An' a gal un - der - neath it a wash her che - mise.
But in - stead look a - roun', oh, me spent ev - 'ry poun'.

Oh, Roo-koom - bine ee - na San - ta Fe,

Roo-koom - bine ee - na San - ta Fe, Oh, Roo-koom - bine.

Here is a bell part to play during section A of "Rookoombine."

How do the tones move?

Bells

C   Bb   A   G

A NEW NOTE

To play a recorder part with
"Rookoombine," you need
a new tone—B$^\flat$.

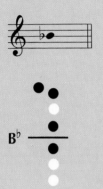

Now play this recorder part. Will you play any tones that leap?

Accompany "Rookoombine" on the Autoharp.
You will need this family of chords.

AN EARLY AMERICAN MELODY

This melody is a favorite of people in many parts of the world. On this recording, Jean Ritchie, the lady in the picture, accompanies the song on a dulcimer. She also sings the first verse as a solo.

As you sing the song, notice how the tones move. Do they step, leap, or repeat?

Amazing Grace

EARLY AMERICAN MELODY   WORDS BY JOHN NEWTON

1. A - maz - ing___ grace how sweet the sound
That saved a___ wretch like me!___
I once___ was___ lost, but now___ am___ found,
Was blind, but___ now I see.___

2. 'Twas grace that taught my heart to fear,
   And grace my fears relieved;
   How precious did that grace appear
   The hour I first believed!

3. Through many dangers, toils, and snares,
   I have already come;

'Tis grace has brought me safe thus far,
And grace will lead me home.

4. The Lord has promised good to me,
   His word my hope secures;
   He will my shield and portion be
   As long as life endures.

A FOLK INSTRUMENT

The dulcimer is a folk instrument from the southern part of the United States. It is used to accompany many songs like "Amazing Grace."

Look at the picture. What do you think Jean Ritchie is using to strum the strings?

Listen for the tones that step, leap, and repeat in the dulcimer part on the recording that was made especially for you.

Notice the many repeated sounds in the accompaniment for verse 4.

STEPS, LEAPS, REPEATS

CHOPSTICKS TRADITIONAL

Play "Chopsticks" as follows on piano or bells.

The keyboard will help you find where to begin.

194

A BIRTHDAY MELODY

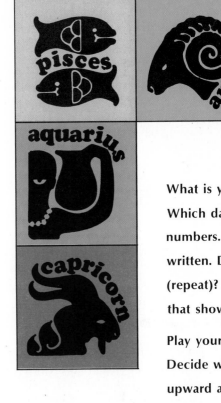

What is your birth date? Which month? Which day? Which year? Write it down by using numbers. Look at the line of numbers you have written. Do you see any number twice in a row (repeat)? Do you see two numbers side by side that show a large interval? A small interval?

Play your number pattern on a melody instrument. Decide which tone will be number 1 and play upward and downward by step or by leap, or repeat a tone as the numbers tell you.

Do you have a zero in your number line? Play it as a percussion sound, or make it silent.

You can vary the pattern. Change the tempo. Change the dynamics. Change the rhythm. Change the starting note. Play the pattern backward.

Think of a way to write down your melody.

Make up a special birthday melody for a friend. Add your own words and give it to your friend as a present.

A MELODY FROM INDIA

Steps, leaps, and repeats are used in melodies from different countries all over the world.

Try singing the song with the recording. Notice how the tones move.

The words of "Namane Kare" mean "Respect your teachers and keep a clean body and mind."

Namane Kare
FOLK SONG FROM INDIA

USED BY PERMISSION OF WILLIAM M. ANDERSON.

Na - ma - ne ka - re cha - tu - re shi - ri gu - ru cha - ra - na,
(Nah-mah-nuh kah-ruh chah-too-ruh shee-ree goo-roo chah-rah-nah,

Ta - ne ma - ne ni - re - ma - le ka - re bha - ve ta - ra - na.
Tah-nuh mah-nuh nee-ruh-mah-luh kah-ruh bhah-vuh tah-rah-nah.

Na - ma - ne ka - re cha - tu - re shi - ri gu - ru cha - ra - na.
Nah-mah-nuh kah-ruh chah-too-ruh shee-ree goo-roo chah-rah-nah.)

In this song from India, an instrument called a *tambura* accompanies the melody. Look at the next page to see a picture of a tambura. Then listen to the recording to hear how it sounds.

low G

high C

high C

low C

To imitate the sound of the tambura, play a drone accompaniment on the Autoharp. Pluck a C and G string at the same time and play throughout the song.

GETTING IT ALL TOGETHER

On this recording you will hear a melody, or theme, that is known all over the world. As you listen, follow the notation of the theme and think of all the things you know about how a melody works. Try to find the answers to these questions:

- How many phrases are there?
- Which phrases have the same, or almost the same, contour?
- How do the tones move in each phrase?

STEPS, LEAPS, REPEATS
TEMPO
METER
REGISTER
RHYTHM PATTERNS
PHRASES
CONTOUR
DYNAMICS
TONE COLOR

Beethoven: *Symphony No. 9 in D Minor*, Movement 4

Theme

HOW FAR CAN YOU GO?

What other musical qualities do you hear on the recording? The words in the graphic at the top of the page will tell you what to listen for.

Try playing the theme on piano, bells, or recorder. It starts on the tone B.

Here are the melodies of some songs that you know.

Part of each melody is missing on the recording.

Listen and decide whether the missing part moves mostly

by step, by leap, or whether the tones repeat.

Listen. Then choose your answer.

---

1 *America*   STEP   LEAP   REPEAT

---

2 *Rookoombine*   STEP   LEAP   REPEAT

---

3 *Rookoombine*   STEP   LEAP   REPEAT

---

4 *The Star-Spangled Banner*   STEP   LEAP   REPEAT

---

5 *Frère Jacques*   STEP   LEAP   REPEAT

---

6 *Reveille*   STEP   LEAP   REPEAT

The Arts: *Exploring New Paths*

A computer helped the artist create this picture.

Look at the top line of drawings from left to right. It shows several things in a row.

Look at the bottom line of drawings from left to right. It shows how an artist can give a feeling of movement from one thing to another.

"Running Cola is Africa 1967/68" by The Computer Technique Group, Japan. Computer Graphic from I.C.A. Exhibition Cybernetic Serendipity; Published by Motif Editions ©.

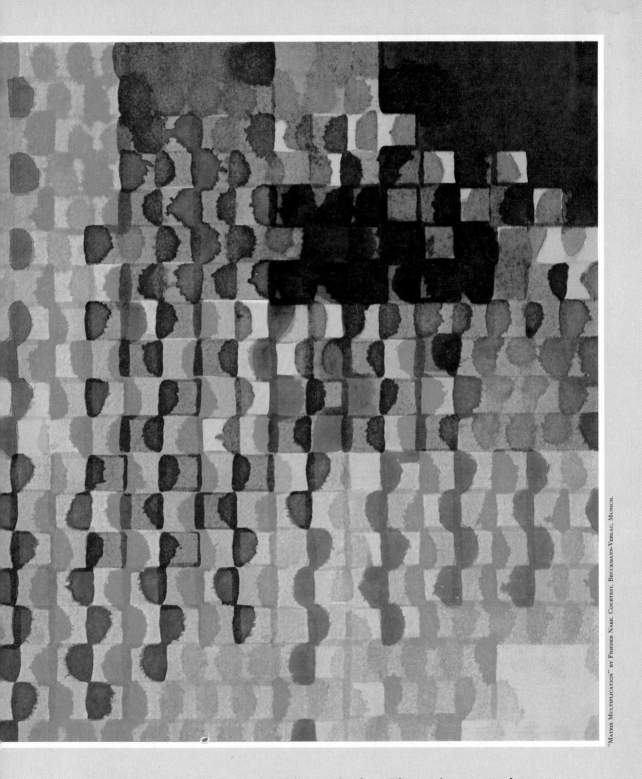

"Matrix Multiplication" by Frieder Nake. Courtesy, Bruckmann-Verlag, Munich.

A computer helped create this work also. The artist wanted to suggest movement from one thing to another. Look at the work from left to right. Try to feel it moving along.

FOLLOW THE CHART

Music moves from moment to moment with sounds and silences. You can feel and hear these as they move along from a beginning to an end. Listen for the sounds and silences in this music.

 Varèse: *Poème électronique*

This chart will help you describe what you heard.

HIGH AND LOW SOUNDS	*LOUD AND SOFT SOUNDS*
UPWARD AND DOWNWARD DIRECTION	*DIFFERENT TONE COLORS*
PAUSES	*THIN AND THICK DENSITY*
FAST AND SLOW MOVEMENT	*WIDE AND NARROW RANGE*

Sounds and silences can be "formed" to do something as they move along from a beginning to an end.

Follow the score on pages 204 and 205 as you listen to *Sound Piece 9*. This piece was composed using a piano melody and a tape recorder.

After you have listened, try creating your own sound piece on a stereo tape recorder. Use voices or instruments or both. The chart below will help you organize your ideas.

Channel I

10″	10″	10″	10″
sound	silence	sound	silence

Now go back to the beginning of your 40-second piece. This time, fill in the silences by recording new material on Channel II. Follow the chart below, or think of something else to do.

Channel I

sound	silence	sound	silence

Channel II

	Play at a different speed.		Slow down the feed reel.

SOUND PIECE 9:
Theme and Tape Recorder "Alteration"

JOYCE BOGUSKY-REIMER

© 1980 JOYCE BOGUSKY-REIMER

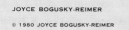

Theme

"Alteration"

Speed Change

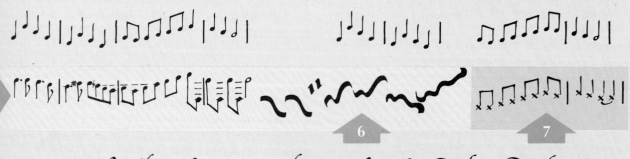

Sound with Sound   *Slowing and Speeding Reel*   *Pinching Tape*

8

10

Speed Change

9

Speed Change

Sound with Sound

11

Speed Change

14

13

15

12

16

Speed Change

Sound with Sound

Speed Change

Meter

A MELODY IN TWO METERS

In some American Indian music you can hear and feel that the sets of beats keep changing from 3 to 2. To help you hear this, listen to the tom-tom accompaniment on the recording.

Muje Mukesin

 OJIBWAY INDIAN TUNE

Mu - je muk - e - sin, aw - yaw - yon, Mu - je muk - e - sin, aw - yaw - yon,

Mu - je muk - e - sin, aw - yaw - yon, Mu - je muk - e - sin, aw - yaw - yon.

Play this pattern to accompany the song. Be certain to stress the first beat—the strong beat—of each measure.

Sometimes sets of three beats and two beats are grouped together in the same measure. When this happens, the music has a meter in 5. Listen to this music. Try to feel the beats grouped in sets of five. Listen for the strong beat at the beginning of each set.

Desmond: *Take Five*

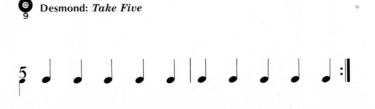

FEELING TWO BEATS PER MEASURE

The words of this song mean "Here it is good and pleasant for brethren to sit together."

Feel the steady beat—two beats per measure—as you listen to the recording.

Hineh Mah Tov
HEBREW FOLK SONG

Hi-neh mah tov u-ma na - im, She-vet a-chim gam ya - chad.

Hi - neh mah_____ tov, She-vet a-chim gam ya - chad.

Play these percussion patterns to accompany "Hineh mah tov."

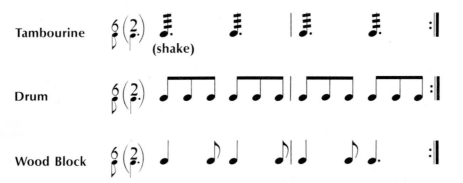

Tambourine (shake)

Drum

Wood Block

You will find these four patterns in "Hineh mah tov." Are any of them used in the railroad song on the next page?

1.
2.
3.
4.

208

Paddy Works on the Railway

IRISH-AMERICAN RAILROAD SONG

9

Look at the rhythm pattern made by the notes in the color box.

Find another place in the song where this pattern is used.

VERSE

SOLO

1. In eigh - teen hun - dred and for - ty - one   I
2. In eigh - teen hun - dred and for - ty - two   I

put   my cor - du - roy breech - es   on,   I   put   my cor - du - roy
left the old___ world for   the new, Oh, spare me the luck___ that

breech - es   on   to   work up - on   the rail - way.
brought   me through   to   work up - on   the rail - way.

REFRAIN

CHORUS

Fil - li - mee - oo - ree - oo - ree - ay,   Fil - li - mee - oo - ree - oo - ree - ay,

Fil - li - mee - oo - ree - oo - ree - ay,   to   work up - on   the rail - way.

3. It's "Pat, do this," and "Pat, do that," without a stocking or cravat,

   And nothing but an old straw hat, while working on the railway. *Refrain*

Sing this countermelody during the refrain.

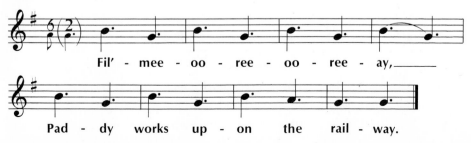

Countermelody

Fil' - mee - oo - ree - oo - ree - ay,_____

Pad - dy works up - on   the rail - way.

A COMPOSER SINGS

Fred Stark, the man who wrote this song, is also a singer. He made this recording especially for you. You can tell from his singing that he and his brother have had some good times together.

Me and My Brother, Oliver Lee

WORDS AND MUSIC BY FRED STARK

© 1972 Fred Stark. © 1979 Eleven Eggs Music, Inc. Reprinted by permission.

1. Most of the time we are hap - py and gay,
2. Leav - ing for school, be gone most of the day,
3. Home-ward we go a - gain, run - ning a - long, The

Laugh - in' and play - in' the hours_____ a - way,
Me and my broth - er, good - by we would say,
mis - chief we're in - to, hope it won't be wrong,

Spend - ing some time in the eve - ning at home with him._____
Laugh - in' and car - ry - in' on all the time with him._____
Soon we are say - in' our prayers at the end of day._____

Up in the morn - ing at break - ing of dawn,
Mak - in' our way through the day, he and I,
Off in - to slum - ber we slip right a - way,

We're hap - py to - geth - er 'most all the day long,_____
I need help with home-work, he'll give it a try,_____
'Cause to - mor - row's an - oth - er won - der - ful day,_____

210

Me and my broth - er, Ol - i - ver Lee,
Me and my broth - er, Ol - i - ver Lee,
With me and my broth - er, Ol - i - ver Lee,

Me and my broth - er, old Ol - i - ver Lee._____
Me and my broth - er, old Ol - i - ver Lee._____
Me and my broth - er, old Ol - i - ver,

Me and my broth - er, old Ol - i - ver Lee.

Me and my broth - er, old Ol - i - ver Lee.

Me and my broth - er, old Ol - i - ver Lee._____

Play these parts to accompany "Me and My Brother, Oliver Lee."

As you play, feel the steady beat divided into threes.

Drum

Tambourine

Listen for the steady beat divided into threes in this music.

 Handel: *Sonata in F*

STRUM AN ACCOMPANIMENT

Silent Night

MUSIC BY FRANZ GRUBER   WORDS BY JOSEPH MOHR

1. Si - lent night, ho - ly night, All is calm,
2. Si - lent night, ho - ly night, Shep - herds quake

all is bright Round yon Vir - gin Moth - er and Child.
at the sight, Glo - ries stream from heav - en a - far,

Ho - ly In - fant so ten - der and mild, Sleep in heav - en - ly
Heav'n - ly hosts sing "Al - le - lu - ia, Christ the Sav - ior is

peace, Sleep in heav - en - ly peace.
born! Christ the Sav - ior is born!"

Play the Autoharp to accompany "Silent Night." Use this
strumming pattern, or create one of your own.

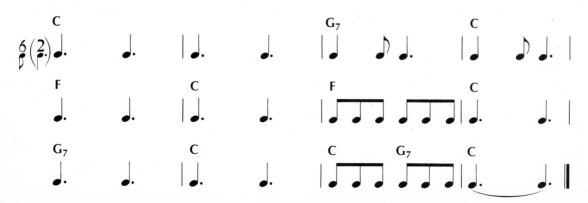

WHAT DO YOU HEAR?   17: Meter 🔊

Can you hear meter in this music? Each time a number is
called, decide whether the meter is in 2, 3, or 5. Listen.
Then choose your answer.

	Meter in	*Meter in*	*Meter in*	
1	2	3	5	Telemann: *Suite in A Minor for Flute and String Orchestra*
2	2	3	5	Britten: *Matinées Musicales*
3	2	3	5	Desmond: *Take Five*
4	2	3	5	Gould: *American Salute*
5	2	3	5	*The Star-Spangled Banner*
6	2	3	5	Tchaikovsky: *Capriccio Italien*
7	2	3	5	Haydn: *String Quartet*, Op. 76

Phrases

As you listen to the recording of this Hawaiian chant, move your arms to show the length of each phrase.

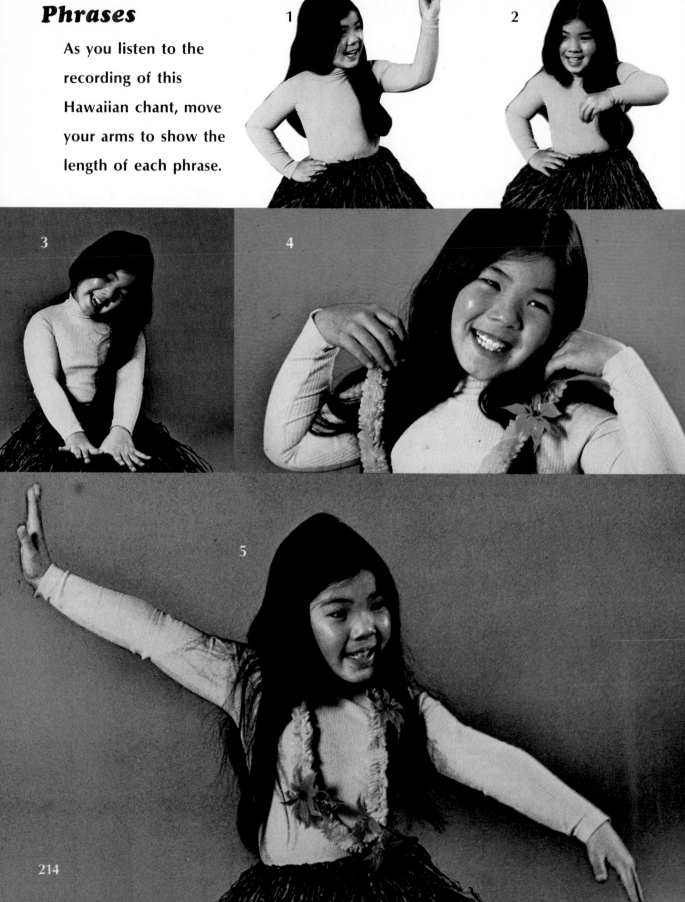

He Mele O Ke Kahuli

FOLK SONG FROM HAWAII

Ka – hu – li a – ku, Ka – hu – li mai,

Ka – hu – li lei u – la, Lei a – ko – le – a,

Ko – le – a, ko – le – a, Ho – i – ka wai

Wai a – ko – le – a, Ko – le – a, ko – le – a.

6

7

215

COMPARING PHRASES

How many phrases are there in this song? Can you discover

what is the same about each phrase?

Harvesting Tea

FOLK SONG FROM JAPAN   ENGLISH WORDS BY RAYMOND MATTHEWS

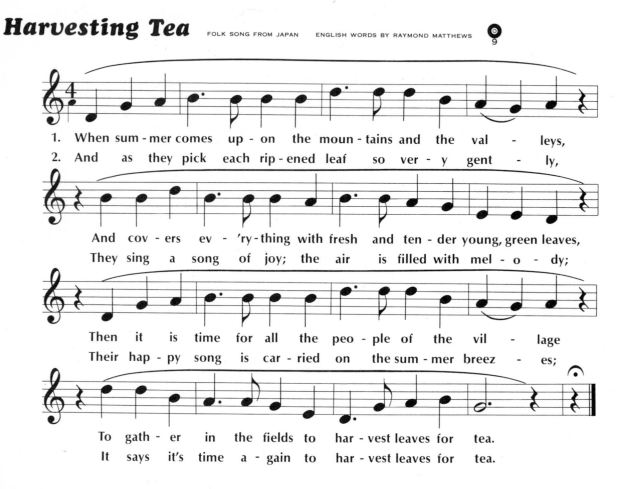

1. When sum - mer comes up - on the moun - tains and the val - leys,
2. And as they pick each rip - ened leaf so ver - y gent - ly,

And cov - ers ev - 'ry - thing with fresh and ten - der young, green leaves,
They sing a song of joy; the air is filled with mel - o - dy;

Then it is time for all the peo - ple of the vil - lage
Their hap - py song is car - ried on the sum - mer breez - es;

To gath - er in the fields to har - vest leaves for tea.
It says it's time a - gain to har - vest leaves for tea.

Play this countermelody as others sing "Harvesting Tea."

Recorder or Bells

LONG PHRASES OR SHORT PHRASES?

By the time Jane gets three hunting dogs, you should be able to join in on the chorus parts.

Will you be singing long phrases, or short phrases? Are the chorus parts the same, or different?

Jane, Jane AMERICAN FOLK SONG

REPRINTED FROM SING OUT! THE FOLK SONG MAGAZINE, 505 EIGHTH AVE., NEW YORK, N.Y. 10018. USED WITH PERMISSION.

SOLO CHORUS SOLO CHORUS

1. Hey, hey,___ Jane, Jane, My Lord-y, Lord, Jane, Jane,

SOLO CHORUS SOLO CHORUS

I'm___ a-gon-na buy, Jane, Jane, Three mock-ing birds, Jane, Jane,

SOLO CHORUS SOLO CHORUS

One___ a-for to whis-tle, Jane, Jane, One___ a-for to sing, Jane, Jane,

SOLO CHORUS SOLO CHORUS

One___ a-for to do, Jane, Jane, Most an-y lit-tle thing, Jane, Jane.

2. Hey, hey, Jane, Jane,
My Lordy, Lord, Jane, Jane,
I'm a-gonna buy, Jane, Jane,
Three hunting dogs, Jane, Jane,
One a-for to run, Jane, Jane,
One a-for to shout, Jane, Jane,
One to talk to, Jane, Jane,
When I go out, Jane, Jane.

3. Hey, hey, . . .
My Lordy, Lord, . . .
I'm a-gonna buy, . . .
Three muley cows, . . .
One a-for to milk, . . .
One to plough my corn, . . .
One a-for to pray, . . .
On Christmas morn, . . .

4. Hey, hey, . . .
My Lordy, Lord, . . .
I'm a-gonna buy, . . .
Three little blue birds, . . .
One a-for to weep, . . .
One a-for to mourn, . . .
One a-for to grieve, . . .
When I am gone, . . .

SAME CONTOUR, DIFFERENT LEVELS

Follow the phrase lines as you listen to this song. Notice especially the short phrases shown in the color boxes. How are they alike? How are they different?

Three White Gulls

FOLK SONG FROM ITALY   ENGLISH WORDS BY MARGUERITE WILKINSON

ORIGINAL TITLE "THE THREE DOVES" BY MARGUERITE WILKINSON FROM BOTSFORD COLLECTION OF FOLK SONGS—VOLUME 3. COPYRIGHT © 1921, 1922 G. SCHIRMER, INC. USED BY PERMISSION.

1. There are three_____ white gulls_____ a - fly - ing;
2. In the waves_____ they dip_____ their soft wings;

There are three_____ white gulls_____ a - fly - ing;
In the waves_____ they dip_____ their soft _____ wings;

There are three_____ white gulls a - fly - ing;_____
In the waves_____ they dip their soft wings;_____

By the sea they cry, By the sea they cry, By the sea they cry.
Then__ soar to the sky, Then__ soar to the sky, Then__ soar to the sky.

There are three_____ white gulls a - fly - ing;_____
In the waves_____ they dip their soft wings;_____

By the sea they cry, By the sea they cry, By the sea they cry.
Then__ soar to the sky, Then__ soar to the sky, Then__ soar to the sky.

SEQUENCES

Nine Red Horsemen

FOLK MELODY FROM MEXICO   WORDS BY ELEANOR FARJEON

10

FROM ELEANOR FARJEON'S POEMS FOR CHILDREN. ORIGINALLY PUBLISHED IN SING FOR YOUR SUPPER BY ELEANOR FARJEON, COPYRIGHT, 1938, BY ELEANOR FARJEON, RENEWED 1966 BY GERVASE FARJEON. BY PERMISSION OF J.B. LIPPINCOTT, PUBLISHERS; AND HAROLD OBER ASSOCIATES, INCORPORATED.

1. I____ saw nine red horse - men ride____ o - ver the plain,
2. Their____ hair streamed be - hind them, their____ eyes were a - shine;
3. Their____ spurs clinked and jin - gled, their____ laugh - ter was gay,

And ____ each gripped his horse ____ by its long flow - ing mane.
They ____ all rode as one man al - though they were nine.
And ____ in the red sun - set they____ gal - loped a - way.

Ho hil - lo, hil - lo, hil - lo ho!   Ho hil - lo, hil - lo, hil - lo ho!

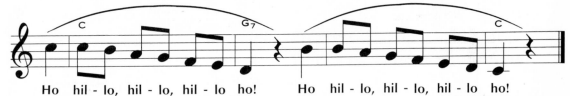

Ho hil - lo, hil - lo, hil - lo ho!   Ho hil - lo, hil - lo, hil - lo ho!

A NEW NOTE

To play an ostinato on recorder,

you need a new tone—low C.

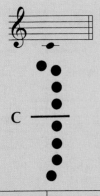

Ostinato (Recorder or Bells)

E

Listen for the sequences in these pieces for keyboard.

10 Handel: *Passepied*   10 Villa-Lobos: *Constante*

CADENCE—STRONG, WEAK

Listen for the strong cadence at the end of each phrase in section A.

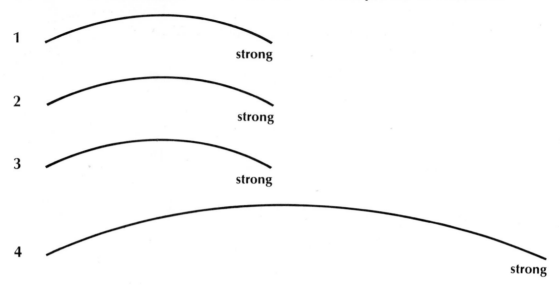

1   strong

2   strong

3   strong

4   strong

Oh, What a Beautiful City
BLACK SPIRITUAL   10

(A) REFRAIN

Oh,   what a beau - ti - ful cit - y, ____

Oh,   what a beau - ti - ful cit - y, ____

Oh,   what a beau - ti - ful cit - y, ____

Twelve gates - a to the cit - y, ____ Hal - le - lu - jah!

220

Listen for the combination of weak and strong cadences in section B.

1 ⌒ weak   2 ⌒ strong

3 ⌒ weak   4 ⌒ strong

5 ⌒ strong

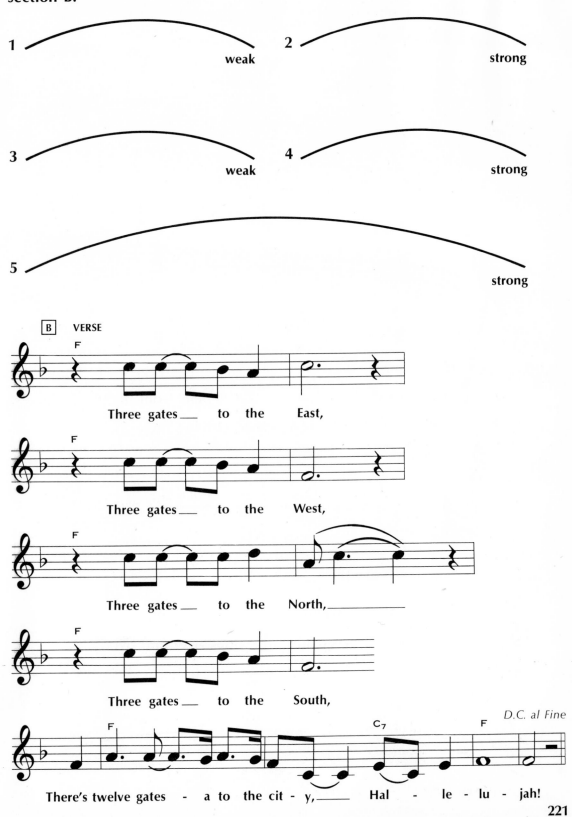

B VERSE

Three gates __ to the East,

Three gates __ to the West,

Three gates __ to the North, _____

Three gates __ to the South,

D.C. al Fine

There's twelve gates - a to the cit - y, ____ Hal - le - lu - jah!

221

EXPERIMENT WITH SOUND AND SILENCE

Choose one of the phrases below. Play each event on the instrument named. "Play" the phrase again, silently.

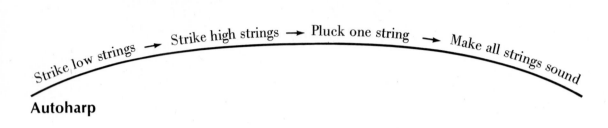

Autoharp

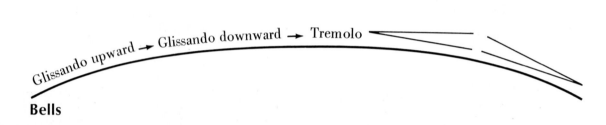

Bells

Glissando upward—Pull mallet across bells from lowest to highest.

Glissando downward—Pull mallet across bells from highest to lowest.

Tremolo—Play any two bells together, striking them

rapidly over and over.

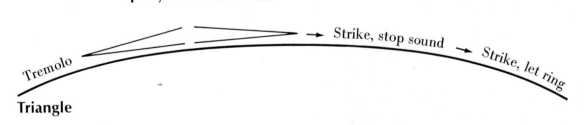

Triangle

Tremolo—With beater inside triangle, use a circular

motion to strike the three sides over and over.

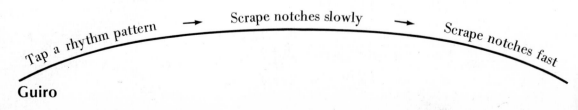

Guiro

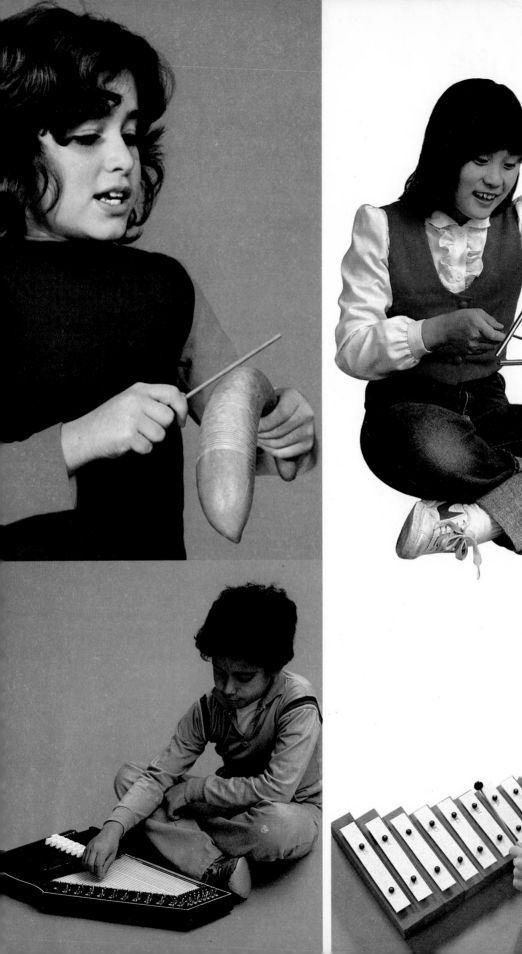

Style: Polynesian

Because people moved from island to island, the music of Polynesia spread from tribe to tribe. Look at the map to see the names of some of the islands. The people there sing and dance the stories and legends they love so well.

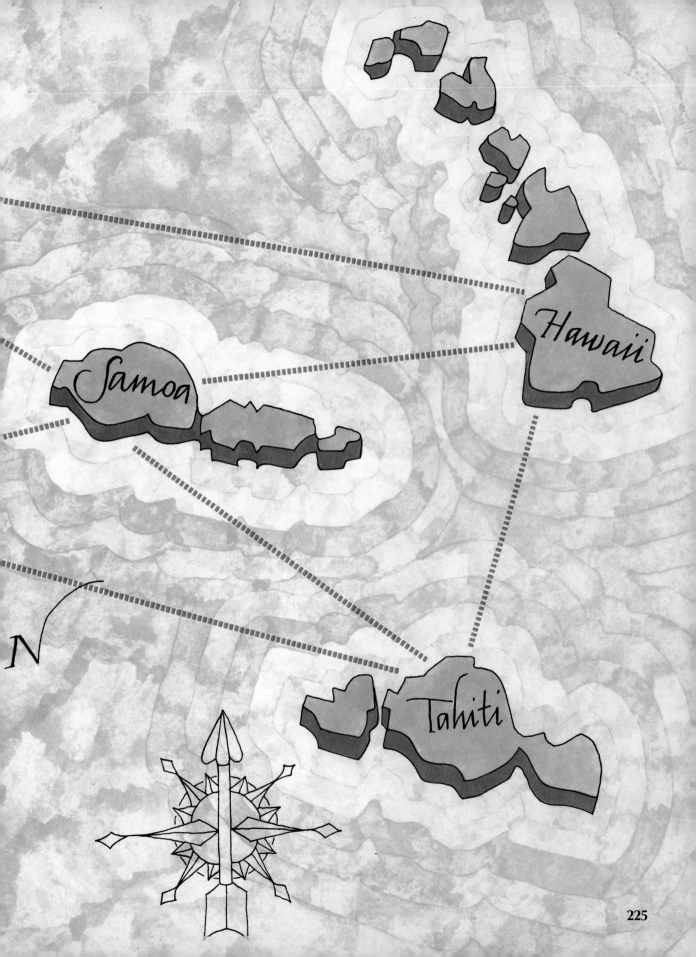

N

Hawaii

Samoa

Tahiti

CHANTS FROM POLYNESIA

Listen to these chants. The first is from Hawaii. The second is from Tahiti.

🔘 *Ai a la o Pele*
10

🔘 *Tahitian Chant*
10

You will find another Polynesian song on page 215 in your book. Play this rhythm pattern on a gourd or ipu as an accompaniment.

hit with heel of hand   hit with finger tips   heel   tip   tip

Polynesian music uses chant, rhythm, and movement to create a style of its own.

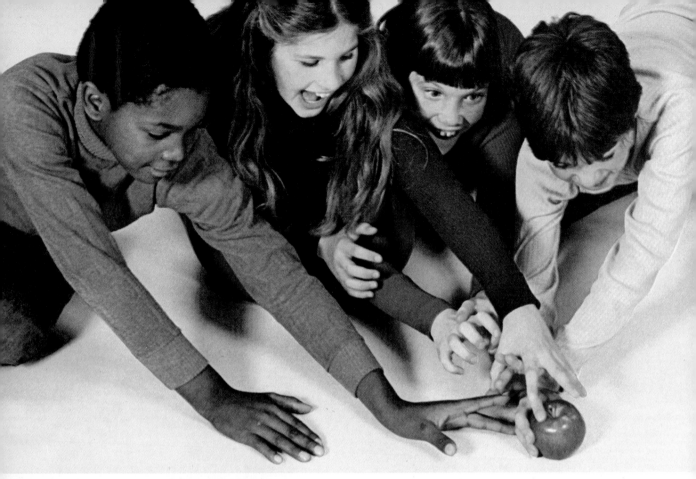

Tonality / Atonality

TONAL CENTER, NO TONAL CENTER

Listen to the bugle call *Reveille*. Try to hear how the music focuses on one important tone.

 Reveille

Now play *Reveille* on the bells D, G, B. As you play, feel the pull toward the tonal center, G.

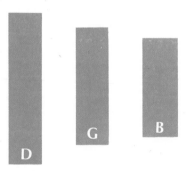

REVEILLE

When you played *Reveille,* you used three different tones.

Now play a melody that uses twelve different tones.

Take the bells from C to B out of the box and arrange them
as follows:

A# A B C# D C D# F E F# G# G

Play the bells from left to right. Use any rhythm you choose.

Is there a pull toward a tonal center in this melody?

Is there a focus on one important tone?

BUGLE CALLS AND FANFARES

Bugle calls and fanfares are often used to announce important events. The first fanfare you will hear was used for many important ceremonies in England several hundred years ago. The second one was used to open the New York State Theater at the Lincoln Center for the Performing Arts in New York City. Which is tonal? Which is atonal?

🔊 Purcell: *Fanfare*
10

🔊 Stravinsky: *Fanfare for Two Trumpets*
10

LISTENING FOR MAJOR AND MINOR

Here are the endings of two songs you know. They each have a pull toward a tonal center. Do they end on the same tone, or on different tones?

1.
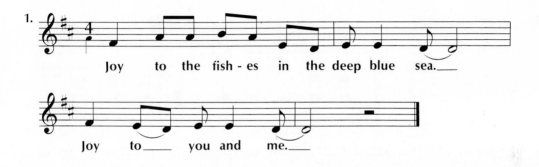

Joy   to the fish - es in the deep blue sea.___

Joy   to___ you and   me.___

2.

Bet - ter keep your hand right   on___ that plow,___

Hold on, hold on, hold on.

Both songs are tonal. Both songs end on D. Yet each song has a different general sound or tonality.

"Joy to the World" has a major tonality.

"Hold On" has a minor tonality.

Each song uses a different arrangement of tones, or scale.

Play these major and minor scales on bells.

MAJOR D E F# G A B C# D

MINOR D E F G A Bb C D

MAJOR OR MINOR?

Listen to the recording of "Chanukah Song." Is the tonality major, or minor?

Playing the Autoharp chords in section A may help you decide.

Chanukah Song

HASIDIC FOLK SONG   ENGLISH WORDS BY ALICE FIRGAU

'Tis the week of Cha - nu - kah, Good cheer it is bring - ing. This
hol - i - day we cel - e - brate in danc - ing and sing - ing. ___

Gath - er round to - geth - er, the ho - ra we'll do;

Then join in a song that our fore - fath - ers knew. But

hush now and come now, The can - dles we light one by

one. Then hear the sto - ry of God and His glo - ry And

how pre - cious free - dom was won.

Listen to the recording. Each time a number is called, choose the word that describes the tonality. Is the music tonal, or atonal? Listen. Then choose your answer.

1   *TONAL*   *ATONAL*   **Prokofiev: *Classical Symphony*, "Gavotte"**

2   *TONAL*   *ATONAL*   **Webern: *Five Movements for String Quartet***

3   *TONAL*   *ATONAL*   **Stravinsky: *Fanfare for Two Trumpets***

4   *TONAL*   *ATONAL*   **Beethoven: *Symphony No. 9***

5   *TONAL*   *ATONAL*   **Purcell: *Fanfare***

6   *TONAL*   *ATONAL*   **Mozart: *Symphony No. 40***

233

LISTENING FOR MAJOR AND PENTATONIC

Play the major scale starting on G. Then play the pentatonic scale.

MAJOR	G	A	B	C	D	E	F♯	G
PENTATONIC	G	A	B		D	E		G

Here are two songs that you know. Sing them to hear which
matches the general sound of the major scale and which
matches the general sound of the pentatonic scale.

"The Frog in the Well," p. 178

"Harvesting Tea," p. 216

Play this pentatonic melody on recorder or bells.

You will need these five tones.

Practice them before you play.

Recorder

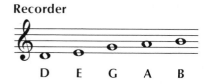

D E G A B

An Iroquois Lullaby   IROQUOIS INDIAN SONG   10

FROM CANADA'S STORY IN SONG BY EDITH FOWKE AND ALAN MILLS. © GAGE PUBLISHING 1965. REPRINTED BY PERMISSION.

Ho, ho,___ wa - ta - nay, Ho, ho,___ wa - ta - nay,

Ho, ho,___ wa - ta - nay, Ki - yo - ke - na, ki - yo - ke - na.

A FIVE-TONE MELODY

This song from China is sung at New Year's celebrations.
The melody is based on the pentatonic scale. Sing it or play it
on recorder or bells. You will need these five tones.

Colorful Boats

FOLK SONG FROM CHINA   ENGLISH VERSION BY CAROL KERR

LISTENING FOR MAJOR AND WHOLE TONE

Look at these scale diagrams. Play the scales on bells.

MAJOR	C	D	E F	G	A	B C
WHOLE TONE	C	D	E	F#	G#	A# C

Play "Frère Jacques" as a major melody, using the tones of the major scale.

FRERE JACQUES   (Major)

Now play "Frère Jacques" as a whole-tone melody, using the tones of the whole-tone scale.

FRERE JACQUES   (Whole Tone)

Each scale has a different general sound. A melody has the same general sound as the scale it is based on.

MAJOR OR WHOLE TONE?

Listen to this song. Is the melody based on a major scale, or a whole-tone scale?

End of Summer
MUSIC BY DAVID EDDLEMAN   WORDS BY SUZANNE SCHMITT

Swim - ming, _ Build - ing cas - tles Out _ of sand _ at the shore.

Till the tide comes wash - ing a - way Sum - mer, _

Sum - mer, _____ Sum - mer. _____

The lyrics of "End of Summer" form a five-line poem called a *cinquain.* The lines of a cinquain follow this pattern of syllables: 2-4-6-8-2.

Swimming, (2)

Building castles (4)

Out of sand at the shore. (6)

Till the tide comes washing away (8)

Summer. (2)

Arrange the bells to match the whole-tone scale shown in the diagram on page 236. Then make up your own whole-tone melody for this poem or for one you have written.

The Arts: *Focus/No Focus*

In some paintings your eyes travel to one important place—a center of interest, or focus.

Which of these paintings has such a focus? Which has not?

GEORGIA O'KEEFFE. THE WHITE FLOWER. (1931.) OIL ON CANVAS. 30 x 36 INCHES. COLLECTION OF THE WHITNEY MUSEUM OF AMERICAN ART. PURCHASE.

In some music your ears hear one tone as most important
(tonal music).

The music comes to rest on that tone.

Some music does not have a tonal center (atonal music).

Listen to these pieces. Which is tonal? Which is atonal?

🎯 10 Webern: *Five Movements for String Quartet*

🎯 10 Mozart: *Divertimento in D*

Texture

CALL CHART 9: Texture 🔟

Listen for the different textures in some music you know.

The chart will help you hear them.

---

1 MELODY ALONE

Amazing Grace

---

2 MELODY WITH COUNTERMELODY

Michael Finnegan

---

3 MELODY WITH CHORDS

Me and My Brother, Oliver Lee

---

4 MELODY SUNG AS A ROUND

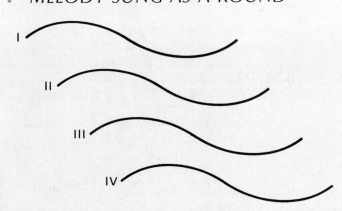

Up the Street the Band Is Marching Down

ONE SONG—DIFFERENT TEXTURES

Sing the melody alone.

This Land Is Your Land

WORDS AND MUSIC BY WOODY GUTHRIE   COUNTERMELODY BY RUTH TUTELMAN

This land is your land,_____ this land is my land,_____

From Ca - li - for - nia_____ to the New York is - land;_____

From the red - wood for - est_____ to the Gulf Stream wa - ters;_____

This land was made for you and me._____

1. As I was walk - ing_____ that rib - bon of high - way,_____

I saw a - bove me_____ that end - less sky - way._____

I saw be - low me_____ that gold - en val - ley,_____

This land was made for you and me._____

2. I've roamed and rambled and I followed my footsteps
   To the sparkling sands of her diamond deserts,
   And all around me a voice was sounding,
   "This land was made for you and me." *Refrain*

3. When the sun comes shining and I was strolling
   And the wheatfields waving and the dust clouds rolling,
   As the fog was lifting a voice was chanting,
   "This land was made for you and me." *Refrain*

Sing the melody with Autoharp accompaniment.

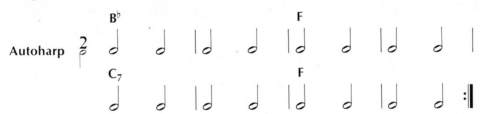

Add this countermelody when you sing the refrain.

COUNTERMELODY (Refrain)

DENSITY: THIN/THICK

When you can sing this song, sing it as a round. The density becomes thicker as each part is added.

Melody Alone   Two-Part Round   Three-Part Round   Four-Part Round

The Ghost of John

WORDS AND MUSIC BY MARTHA GRUBB

I — Have you seen the ghost of John?

II — Long white bones with the skin all gone,____

III — Oo, oo,____

IV — Would - n't it be chil - ly with no skin on!

For an even thicker density, add the parts for bells or recorder to the singing.

Bells or Recorder

1. (4 times)

2. (4 times)

CHANGE THE TEXTURE

Listen to the recording. What instruments accompany this hymn of thanksgiving?

Add a tom-tom beat to accompany the melody.

Psalm of Thanksgiving

DAKOTA INDIAN HYMN   MUSICAL SETTING BY CARLTON YOUNG

ENGLISH WORDS BY PHILIP FRAZIER

1. Man - y and great, O God, are Thy things, Mak - er of earth and sky;___ Thy hands have set the heav - ens with stars; Thy fin - gers spread the moun-tains and plains.___ Lo, at Thy word the wa - ters were formed; Deep seas o - bey Thy voice.

2. Grant un - to us com-mu - nion with Thee, Thou star - a - bid - ing One;___ Come un - to us and dwell with___ us With Thee are found the gifts of___ life.___ Bless us with life that has no___ end, E - ter - nal life with Thee.

Change the texture by adding one or both of these parts.

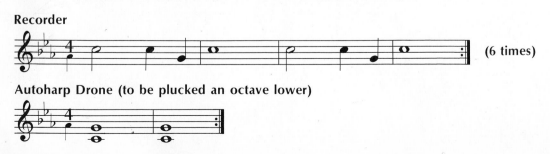

Recorder

(6 times)

Autoharp Drone (to be plucked an octave lower)

A SONG IN TWO TEXTURES

Perform this song two ways:

1. as a melody alone
2. as a melody with chords

He's Got the Whole World in His Hands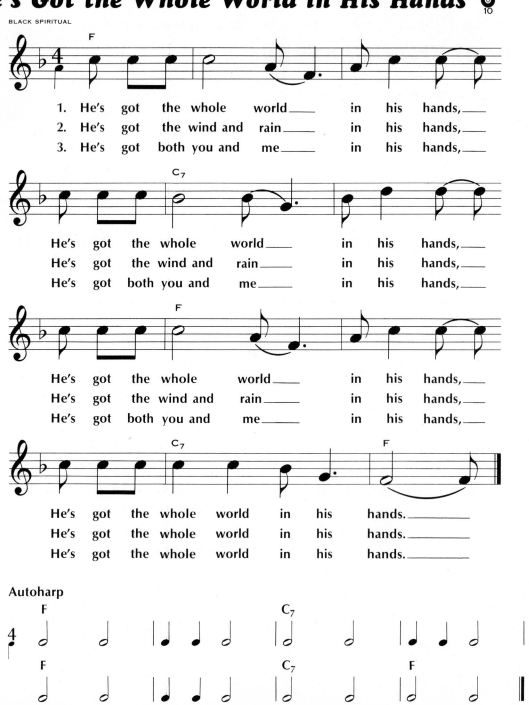

BLACK SPIRITUAL

1. He's got the whole world___ in his hands,___
2. He's got the wind and rain___ in his hands,___
3. He's got both you and me___ in his hands,___

He's got the whole world___ in his hands,___
He's got the wind and rain___ in his hands,___
He's got both you and me___ in his hands,___

He's got the whole world___ in his hands,___
He's got the wind and rain___ in his hands,___
He's got both you and me___ in his hands,___

He's got the whole world in his hands._____
He's got the whole world in his hands._____
He's got the whole world in his hands._____

Autoharp

WHAT DO YOU HEAR? 19: Texture

Listen to this music. Sometimes you will hear a melody with guitar accompaniment. The density of the sound will be thin. Sometimes you will hear a vocal or instrumental countermelody along with the melody and accompaniment. The density of the sound will be thicker. Each time a number is called, choose the answer that describes the texture you hear.

Makem: *Winds of Morning*

1	MELODY WITH ACCOMPANIMENT THIN DENSITY	COUNTERMELODY ADDED THICKER DENSITY
2	MELODY WITH ACCOMPANIMENT THIN DENSITY	COUNTERMELODY ADDED THICKER DENSITY
3	MELODY WITH ACCOMPANIMENT THIN DENSITY	COUNTERMELODY ADDED THICKER DENSITY
4	MELODY WITH ACCOMPANIMENT THIN DENSITY	COUNTERMELODY ADDED THICKER DENSITY
5	MELODY WITH ACCOMPANIMENT THIN DENSITY	COUNTERMELODY ADDED THICKER DENSITY
6	MELODY WITH ACCOMPANIMENT THIN DENSITY	COUNTERMELODY ADDED THICKER DENSITY

The Arts: Density

These two paintings are by the same artist. What do you notice about the top part of each? What do you notice about the bottom part of each?

The density of what you see is an important part of how a painting feels.

TANGUY, YVES. MULTIPLICATION DES ARCS, 1954. OIL ON CANVAS, 40 x 60". COLLECTION, THE MUSEUM OF MODERN ART, NEW YORK, MRS. SIMON GUGGENHEIM FUND.

Music has density, too. Listen to two pieces by the same composer. What do you notice about the density of each one?

Copland: *Statements*

Copland: *Music for a Great City*

Density in painting can be made by having open spaces (thin) or by crowding many things into a space (thick).

Density in music can be made by having only a few sounds (thin) or by piling up sounds together (thick).

Each art creates a feeling of thin or thick in its own way.

249

Singing from Shore to Shore

Away for Rio!

SEA SHANTEY

Sailors sang as they worked on the old sailing ships. The shanteyman set the rhythm for the work with his solo.

SOLO

1. Oh, the an-chor is weighed and the sails they are set,
2. We've a jol-ly good ship and a jol-ly good crew,
3. Oh,— say, were you ev-er in Ri - o Grande?

CHORUS

A - way——— for Ri - o!

SOLO

The gals that we're leav - ing we'll nev - er for - get,
A jol - ly good mate and a good skip - per too,
It's there that the riv - ers run down gold - en sand,

CHORUS

For we're bound for Ri - o Grande!———

REFRAIN

CHORUS

And a-way——— for Ri - o! Aye——— for Ri - o!

SOLO

So fare ye well,——— my bon - ny young girl,

CHORUS

We are bound for Ri - o Grande!———

Down the Ohio

RIVER SHANTEY

As our country grew, riverboats carried families down the Ohio to the Mississippi. From there, they sailed up the Missouri to start a new life in the West.

As you listen to the recording, use your arm to outline the movement of the paddle wheels on the old riverboats.

The riv-er is up and the chan-nel is deep.

The wind is stead-y and strong, ___

Oh, won't we have a jol-ly good time

As we go sail-ing a-long.

B REFRAIN

MELODY
Down the riv-er, Oh, down the riv-er, Oh,

down the riv-er we go - o - o.

Down the riv - er, Oh, down the riv - er, Oh,

down the O - hi - o! _____

Green Grow the Lilacs AMERICAN FOLK SONG

When people moved around from one place to another, they
always "packed" their favorite songs.

1. Oh, green grow the li - lacs all spark - ling with dew,
2. On top of the moun - tain where green li - lacs grow,

How sad was the day when I part - ed from you,
And down in the val - ley where bright wa - ters flow,

But at our next meet - ing our love we'll re - new,
We'll meet there to - geth - er our love to re - new,

We'll change the green li - lacs for the Or - e - gon blue.
And change the green li - lacs for the Or - e - gon blue.

Norwegian Mountain Dance

FOLK SONG FROM NORWAY

ENGLISH WORDS BY MARGARET MARKS

When people from other lands came to our shores, they
brought their favorite songs and dances.

There is a legend that this dance represents two mountain
climbers and their guide exploring the mountains of Norway.

You stamp and step spright - ly, Hold hand - ker - chief tight - ly,
To do this dance right - ly and make it look sight - ly

Just stamp, two, three, stamp, two, three; Now you've be - gun.
Just stamp, two, three, stamp, two, three; Join in the fun.

Un - der goes num - ber one, Two fol - lows un - der one,

Three fol - lows two, Then comes one and you're done.

As you listen to the recording, do this tap-clap pattern all
through the song.

tap R.   clap   clap   tap L.   clap   clap
knee   knee

Night Herding Song

A big part of the cowhand's job is to quiet the dogies—the motherless calves.

1. Oh, slow up, do - gies, quit rov - ing a - round,
2. I've cir - cle herd - ed and night herd - ed too,

You have wan - dered and tram - pled all o - ver the ground;
But to keep you to - geth - er, that's what I can't do;

Oh, graze a - long, do - gies, and feed kind - a slow,
My horse is leg wea - ry, and I'm aw - ful tired,

And don't for - ev - er be on the go. Oh,
But if you get a - way, I am sure to get fired. Bunch

move slow, do - gies, move slow, ___ Hi - oo, hi - oo, ___ hi - oo! ___
up, lit - tle do - gies, bunch up, ___ Hi - oo, hi - oo, ___ hi - oo! ___

3. Oh, lie still, dogies, since you have lain down,

Stretch away out on the big open ground;

Snore loud, little dogies, and drown the wild sound,

That will all go away when the day rolls round.

Lie still, little dogies, lie still. Hi-oo, hi-oo, hi-oo!

Santy Anno

SEA SHANTEY

In the days of the forty-niners, cross-country travel was still slow and hard. Some people got to California by sailing around Cape Horn.

SOLO
1. We're sail - ing down the riv - er from Liv - er - pool,
2. She's a fast___ clip - per ship___ and a bully good crew,

CHORUS
SOLO
Heave a - way, San - ty An - no;___ A - round Cape Horn to
Heave a - way, San - ty An - no;___ A down-East Yan - kee for her

CHORUS
Fris - co Bay, All___ on the plains of Mex - i - co.
cap - tain, too. All___ on the plains of Mex - i - co.___

REFRAIN
So heave her up and a - way we'll go, Heave a -

way,___ San - ty An - no,___ Heave her up and a -

way we'll go, All___ on the plains of Mex - i - co.___

3. There's plenty of gold,
   so I've been told,
Heave away, Santy Anno;
There's plenty of gold,
   so I've been told,
Way out west to Californio.

4. Back in the days
   of Forty-nine,
Heave away, Santy Anno;
Those are the days
   of the good old times,
All on the plains of Mexico.

256

The Railroad Cars Are Coming

AMERICAN FOLK SONG

Clipper ships were slow in bringing people and supplies to the West. A railroad was needed to bring East and West together. Building the railroad across the Rocky Mountains was a great achievement. It is celebrated in song and story.

1. The great Pa - cif - ic rail - way   For Cal - i - for - nia hail!
2. The prai - rie dogs in dog - town,   The rat - tle-snake and quail

Bring on   the lo - co - mo - tive,   Lay down the i - ron rail;
Will see   the cars a - com - ing,   Just fly - ing down the rail.

A - cross   the roll - ing prai - ries, Through moun - tain val - leys grand,
A - mid   the pur - ple sage-brush,   The an - te-lope will stand,

REFRAIN

The   rail - road   cars   are com - ing,_____ hum - ming_____
While

Through_____ the prai - rie land.   The rail-road cars   are com - ing,_____

hum - ming_____ Through_____   the   prai - rie land.

Home on the Range

This is one of the best-known and best-loved cowboy songs of all times.

How does this cowboy feel about his home on the range? To find out, read the words of the song.

1. Oh, give me a home where the buf - fa - lo roam,
2. How of - ten at night when the heav - ens are bright
3. Oh, I love those wild flowers in this dear land of ours,

Where the deer and the an - te - lope play,_____
With the lights from the glit - ter - ing stars,_____
The_____ cur - lew I love to hear scream,_____

Where sel - dom is heard a dis - cour - ag - ing word,
Have I stood there a - mazed and_____ asked as I gazed,
And I love the white rocks and the an - te - lope flocks,

And the skies are not cloud - y all day._____
If their glo - ry ex - ceeds that of ours._____
That_____ graze on the moun - tain - tops green._____

REFRAIN

Home, home on the range,_____ Where the

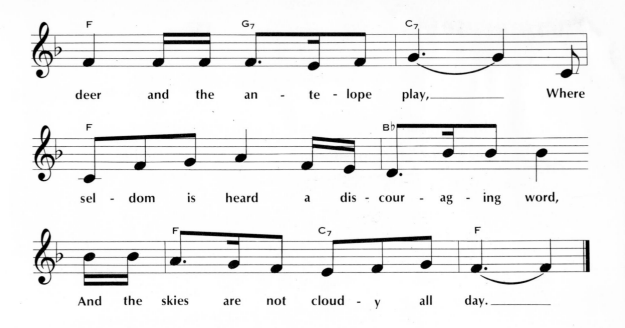

deer and the an - te - lope play, _____ Where

sel - dom is heard a dis - cour - ag - ing word,

And the skies are not cloud - y all day. _____

ADD A COUNTERMELODY

Here is a countermelody to sing with the refrain of "Home on the Range."

Home, home on the range, _____ Where the

deer and the an - te - lope play, _____ Where

sel - dom is heard a dis - cour - ag - ing word, And the

skies are not cloud - y all day. _____

Sacramento

WORDS TRADITIONAL   MUSIC BY STEPHEN FOSTER

In the old days, some of the people who went to California traveled by sea. Sailors on the ships sang these words to a tune by Stephen Foster. The forty-niners learned the shantey and took it ashore, and into the goldfields.

SOLO ... *CHORUS*

1. We've formed our band and we are well manned, Doo - da, doo - da!
2. Where the gold - en ore is rich in store,

SOLO ... *CHORUS*

To jour-ney a - far to the Prom-ised Land, Doo - da, doo - da, day!
On the banks of the Sac - ra - men - to shore,

REFRAIN

CHORUS

Blow, boys, blow, To Cal - i - for - nia go!

There's plen - ty of gold, so I've been told, On the banks of the Sac - ra - men - to!

3. As the gold is thar most anywhar, . . .

   And they dig it out with an iron bar, . . .

   Refrain

4. And whar 'tis thick, with a spade or pick, . . .

   They can take out lumps as heavy as a brick, . . .

   Refrain

260

Abalone

FOLK SONG FROM CALIFORNIA

Many songs grew out of the work people did. The kind of work they did often depended on where they lived.

This folk song is about the abalone, a large shellfish found on the West Coast.

1. In Mon - te - rey   the peo - ple say, "We feed the   laz - za - ro - ni;
2. Oh, some folks boast   of quail   on   toast, Be - cause they think it's   tone - y;

On   car - a - mels and cock - le   shells and hunks of   ab - a - lo - ne."
But   my   big   cat gets nice and   fat   on hunks of   ab - a - lo - ne.

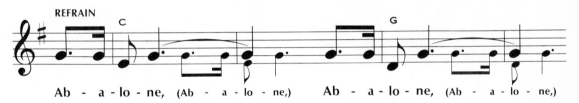

REFRAIN

Ab - a - lo - ne, (Ab - a - lo - ne,)   Ab - a - lo - ne, (Ab - a - lo - ne,)

Ab - a - lo - ne, (Ab - a - lo - ne,)   And hunks of ab - a - lo - ne.

3. I telegraph my better half
   By Morse or by Marconi;
   But when in need of greater speed
   I send an abalone.

4. Our naval hero, best of all,
   His name was Pauley Joney;
   He sailed the sea just as he pleased,
   But he never ate abalone.

The Jasmine Flower

FOLK SONG FROM CHINA   ENGLISH WORDS ADAPTED BY JULIA BINGHAM
11

When people came to our shores, they brought some of their instruments with them. What instruments could you use to accompany this song of friendship from China?

1. See____ this branch____ of____ sweet - est____ flow'rs,

Plucked____ at morn____ from____ dew - y____ bow'rs;

Sent with love____ to greet me, Breath - ing friend - ship sweet.

2. Take this branch of jasmine flow'rs,
   Plucked at morn from dewy bow'rs;
   Given with love to greet you,
   Breathing friendship sweet.

Organize an orchestra for "The Jasmine Flower."

Mallet Instruments

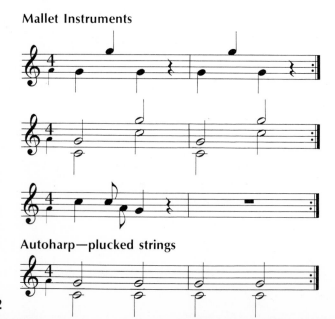

Autoharp—plucked strings

262

The First of January (Uno de Enero)

FOLK SONG FROM MEXICO

FROM CANTEMOS EN ESPAGNOL ARRANGED BY MAX AND BEATRICE KRONE. ©1961 MAX AND BEATRICE KRONE PUBLISHING CO. REPRINTED BY PERMISSION OF NEIL A. KJOS MUSIC COMPANY.

On the seventh of July, people of Spanish origin sing this song to celebrate the fiesta in honor of the Spanish Saint Fermín.

First of the first month, sec-ond of the sec-ond month, Third of the
U - no de e - ne - ro, dos___ de fe - bre - ro, tres___ de

third, and fourth of the fourth; Fifth of the fifth month, sixth of the
mar - zo, cua - tro de a - bril, cin - co de ma - yo, seis___ de

sixth month, Sev - enth of Ju - ly is San Fer - mín.
ju - nio, sie - te de ju - lio, San Fer - mín.

La, la, la, la, la, la, la, Tam-bour-ine's brok-en, we can-not play it.
¿quién___ ha ro - to la pan - de - re - ta?

La, la, la, la, la, la, la, If you broke it, you must re - place it.
el que la ha ro - to la pa - ga - rá.___

Choose one of these parts to play throughout section A.

Hand claps

Tambourine

263

The Returning Hunter

ESKIMO SONG   ENGLISH WORDS BY ELIZABETH WHALEY

11

From the Sixth Annual Report of the Bureau of American Ethnology, Washington, D.C.

Northern Alaska has long been the home of the Eskimos. They
live and work together in small family communities. They
provide their own entertainment by making up poetry and
songs.

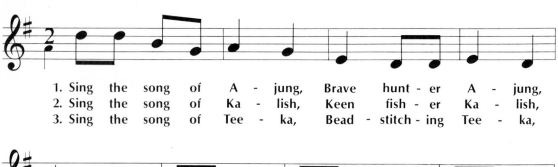

1. Sing the song of A - jung, Brave hunt - er A - jung,
2. Sing the song of Ka - lish, Keen fish - er Ka - lish,
3. Sing the song of Tee - ka, Bead - stitch - ing Tee - ka,

Brave hunt - er, bold and strong. Hunts for po - lar bear at night,
Keen fish - er, quick and true. In his kay - ak small and frail,
Bead - stitch - ing red on white, Sews a par - ka gay and bright,

Sends his spear in speed - y flight,
Braves the sea and wind and hail,
Mak - ing par - ka warm and light.

Hunt - ing car - i - bou, he shows no fright,
Spear - ing fish and ev - en gi - ant whale,
Sew - ing beads of red on hide of white,

O A - jung, *Yai!*
O Ka - lish, *Yai!*
O Tee - ka, *Yai!*

Roll On, Columbia

WORDS BY WOODY GUTHRIE

MUSIC BASED ON "GOODNIGHT. IRENE" BY HUDDIE LEDBETTER & JOHN LOMAX

What rivers of the Northwest are mentioned in this song? Can you find them on a map?

1. Green Doug - las fir where the wa - ters cut through,
2. Oth - er big rivers add___ pow - er to you,

Down her wild moun - tains and can - yons she flew.
Yak - i - ma, Snake, and the Klick - i - tat, too.

Ca - na - di - an North - west to the o - cean so blue,
___ Sand - y, Wil - lam - ette, and the Hood Riv - er, too,

Roll on, Co - lum - bia, roll on.___

REFRAIN
COUNTERMELODY

Roll on,___ Co - lum - bia, roll on. Roll on,___ Co -

lum - bia, roll on. Your pow - er is turn - ing our

dark - ness to dawn, Roll on, Co - lum - bia, roll on.___

265

Recorder Fingering Chart

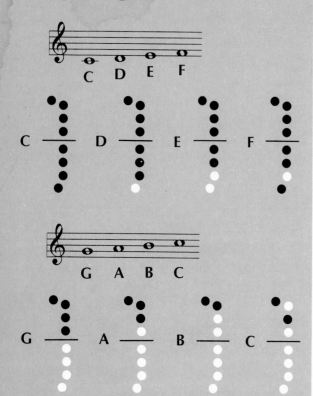

C D E F

C D E F

G A B C

G A B C

D E F

D E F

F♯ B B♭ C♯
(alt)

F♯ B B♭ C♯

Glossary

accent A single tone or chord louder than those around it

accompaniment Music that supports the sound of a solo performer

atonal Music in which no single tone is a "home base" or "resting place"

ballad In music, a song that tells a story

beat A repeating pulse that can be felt in some music

cadence A group of chords or notes at the end of a phrase or piece that gives a feeling of pausing or finishing

chord Three or more different tones played or sung together

chord pattern An arrangement of chords into a small grouping, usually occurring often in a piece

cluster A group of tones very close together performed at the same time; used mostly in modern music

composer A person who makes up pieces of music by putting sounds together in his or her own way

contour The "shape" of a melody, made by the way it moves upward and downward in steps and leaps, and by repeated tones

contrast Two or more things that are different. In music, slow is a *contrast* to fast; section A is a *contrast* to section B.

countermelody A melody that is played or sung at the same time as the main melody

density The thickness or thinness of sound

drone An accompaniment made up of a tone or tones that are repeated or sustained throughout a piece of music

dynamics The loudness and softness of sound

elements The parts out of which whole works of art are made: for example, music uses the *elements* melody, rhythm, texture, tone color, form; painting uses line, color, space, shape, etc.

ensemble A group of players or singers

form The overall plan of a piece of music

ground A melody pattern repeated over and over in the bass (lowest part) of a piece, while other things happen above it

harmony Two or more tones sounding at the same time

improvisation Making up music as it is being performed; often used in jazz

measure A grouping of beats set off by bar lines

melody A line of single tones that move upward, downward, or repeat

melody pattern An arrangement of pitches into a small grouping, usually occurring often in a piece

meter The way the beats of music are grouped, often in sets of two or in sets of three

notes Symbols for sound in music

octave The distance of eight steps from one tone to another that has the same letter name. On the staff these steps are shown by the lines and spaces. When notes are an *octave* apart, there are eight lines and spaces from one note to the other.

pattern In the arts, an arrangement of an element or elements into a grouping, usually occurring often in the work (*see* elements)

phrase A musical "sentence." Each *phrase* expresses one thought. Music is made up of *phrases* that follow one another in a way that sounds right.

pitch The highness or lowness of a tone

range In a melody, the span from the lowest tone to the highest tone

register The pitch location of a group of tones (*see* pitch). If the group of tones are all high sounds, they are in a high *register*. If the group of tones are all low sounds, they are in a low *register*.

repetition Music that is the same, or almost the same, as music that was heard earlier

rests Symbols for silences in music

rhythm The way movement is organized in a piece of music, using beat, no beat, long and short sounds, meter, accents, no accents, tempo, syncopation, etc.

rhythm pattern A pattern of long and short sounds

scale An arrangement of pitches from lower to higher according to a specific pattern of intervals. Major, minor, pentatonic, and whole-tone are four kinds of scales. Each one has its own arrangement of pitches.

sequence The repetition of a melody pattern at a higher or lower pitch level

staff A set of five horizontal lines on which music notes are written

style The overall effect a work of art makes by the way its elements are used (*see* elements). When works of art use elements similarly, they are said to be "in the same style."

syncopation An arrangement of rhythm in which prominent or important tones begin on weak beats or weak parts of beats, giving a catchy, "off-balance" movement to the music

tempo The speed of the beat in a piece of music (*see* beat)

texture The way melody and harmony go together: a melody alone, two or more melodies together, or a melody with chords

theme An important melody that occurs several times in a piece of music

tonal Music that focuses on one tone that is more important than the others—a "home base" or "resting" tone

tone color The special sound that makes one instrument or voice sound different from another

triplet A rhythm pattern made by dividing a beat into three equal sounds

variation Music that is repeated but changed in some important way

vibration Back-and-forth motion that makes sound

Index

Acknowledgments

Credit and appreciation are due publishers and copyright owners for use of the following.

"Crossing" from LETTER FROM A DISTANT LAND by Philip Booth. Copyright 1953 by Philip Booth. Originally appeared in The New Yorker. Reprinted by permission of Viking Penguin Inc.

"Geranium" by Mary Ellen Solt from FLOWERS IN CONCRETE by Fine Arts Department, University of Indiana © 1966. Reprinted by permission of Mary Ellen Solt.

"Slowly" from THE WANDERING MOON by James Reeves. Used by permission of the publisher, William Heinemann Ltd.

"Tom and Joe" from AWAY AND AGO by David McCord. Copyright © 1968, 1971, 1972, 1973, 1974 by David McCord. Used by permission of Little, Brown, and Co.

"Windy Winter Rain . . ." by Shisei-Jo, from JAPANESE HAIKU, p. 57. Copyright © 1955 Peter Pauper Press, Inc. Reprinted by permission.

Picture Credits

Cover: Silver Burdett

2: *t.l.* Silver Burdett; *t.r.* Erich Bach; *b.* Owen Franken from Stock, Boston. 3: Dan De Wilde for Silver Burdett. 8, 11: Silver Burdett. 12: Dr. E. R. Degginger. 12–13: David Austen from Stock, Boston. 13: Nicholas Devore III from Bruce Coleman, Inc. 17–26: Silver Burdett. 34: Peter Menzel from Stock, Boston. 35: Victoria Beller-Smith for Silver Burdett. 38: Erich Hartmann from Magnum. 44–45: Victoria Beller-Smith for Silver Burdett. 46: Dan De Wilde for Silver Burdett. 48: Victoria Beller-Smith for Silver Burdett. 49: *t.l.* Victoria Beller-Smith for Silver Burdett; *t.r.* Curt Gunther from Camera 5; *b.l.* Victoria Beller-Smith for Silver Burdett; *b.r.* Opera News from The Granger Collection. 50: © 1973 Keith Gunnar from Bruce Coleman, Inc. 51: Erich Hartmann from Magnum. 66: *t.* Jay Lyons from DPI; *b.* Burk Uzzle from Magnum. 67: Jonathan Wright from Bruce Coleman, Inc. 68–71: Victoria Beller-Smith for Silver Burdett. 73: Silver Burdett. 89: *t., m.* Dr. William Anderson; *b.* Silver Burdett. 94: Costa Manos from Magnum. 112, 116–117: Victoria Beller-Smith for Silver Burdett. 117: *b.* Dr. E. R. Degginger. 119: Silver Burdett. 125: Verlon L. Stone. 130: Silver Burdett. 134: © Harald Sund. 135: *t.l.* Burk Uzzle from Magnum; *b.l.* R. Archibald from Shostal Associates; *r.* Art Sokoloff from DPI. 160: Farrell Grehan from Photo Researchers, Inc. 166–174: Silver Burdett. 176–177, 178: Victoria Beller-Smith for Silver Burdett. 180: *t.* Aldo Durazzi; *b.* Steinway & Sons. 181: Silver Burdett. 182: *t.* Victoria Beller-Smith for Silver Burdett; *b.* Silver Burdett. 185: Silver Burdett. 186: Eric Carle from Shostal. 187: Ernst Haas from Magnum. 188: *t.* H. Fay from Shostal; *m.* Rudi Schonbeck; *b.* Nicholas Devore III from Bruce Coleman, Inc. 191: Silver Burdett. 193: George Pickow. 197: Dr. William Anderson. 206–215: Victoria Beller-Smith for Silver Burdett. 219, 223: Silver Burdett. 224–225: Karen Ackoff. 226: R. B. Goodman from Black Star. 226–227: N. Myres from Bruce Coleman, Inc. 228, 229: Silver Burdett. 230: J. Alex Langley from DPI. 239: "Tondo 1951" James Brooks. Private Collection, New York City. 240: Silver Burdett. 250: *t.* Matt Greene; *b.* Victoria Beller-Smith for Silver Burdett.

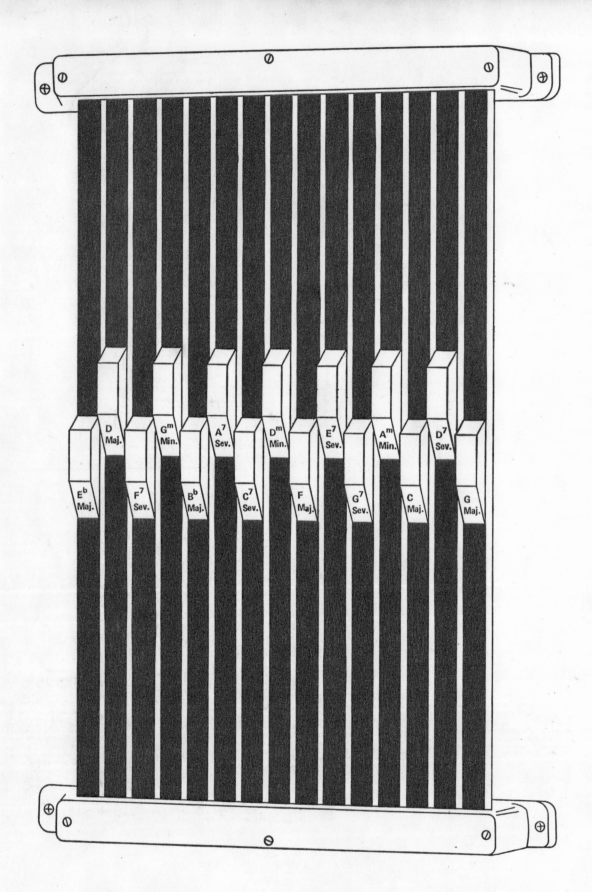